WHAT WOMEN
REALLY ~~WANT~~ NEED

EDITED BY *Lesley Ramsay*

What women really ~~want~~ *need:*
Women talk about Contentment, Love and Forgiveness
This UK edition published by
The Good Book Company Ltd
Elm House, 37 Elm Road
New Malden, Surrey KT3 3HB
Tel: 0845 225 0880; Fax: 0845 225 0990
email: admin@thegoodbook.co.uk
website: www.thegoodbook.co.uk

© Evangelism Ministries, Sydney, Australia 2005.
Website: www.evangelismministries.org.au

Unless otherwise indicated, all Scripture quotations are taken from the Holy Bible:
New International Version. Copyright © 1973, 1978, 1984 by International Bible
Society.

ISBN 1-904889-60-3

Cover design and typesetting by Lankshear Design

Printed and bound in Great Britain by Bookmarque Ltd, Croydon

Contents

Introduction
What women really want

*T*here is a fascinating interchange in the first episode of *Desperate Housewives* – a dark comedy about the lives of a group of women living on Wisteria Lane, somewhere in upmarket suburbia. Gabrielle is the attractive ex-model housewife, and in one scene she has a conversation with John, the gardener, with whom she is having an affair.

He asks her why she married her husband, and she replies, "Because he promised to give me everything I've ever wanted."

He: "Well, did he?"

She: "Yes."

He: "Then why aren't you happy?"

She: "It turns out I wanted all the wrong things."

Maybe someone has given you this book, or perhaps you have picked it up, intrigued by the title.

What *do* women want? What do *you* want? Will the things you want make you happy? Can they provide deep-down happiness and contentment? I hope they do, but what if they turn out to be the wrong things?

The women who have written this book have the same longings and desires as you. They have struggled with unsatisfying relationships, out-of-control diaries, a famine of forgiveness, poor self-esteem, uncertainty and guilt. They have searched for that elusive 'something' that will be the answer to those great longings. But in the end they have all come to see that there is more than 'something': there is a person.

This book, like any other, may be read in its entirety in one or a few reading sessions. If that is the way you like to read, then please do, and enjoy! However, you may prefer to dip in and out. Each chapter stands alone, although they do build to a climax at the end. I hope that you will eventually read all of it.

There are references to the Bible throughout the book. These have been printed in the text for you. However, this may whet your appetite to read more of the Bible, so some suggestions as to where to begin have been provided in the concluding chapter.

I have included four personal stories in the book. Here, four ordinary women (and one brave man!) share how they discovered what they really wanted. And needed.

I hope they lead you to the person who is at the centre of this book: Jesus.

Lesley Ramsay
APRIL, 2005

Spirituality
Gillian Davis

*M*y days of rushing into the local off-licence flustered and overwhelmed are over.

In the past, when guests were almost at the door, I would frantically run to the counter and immediately show my ignorance by asking for a "really, *really* good bottle of white wine… for under £5.00". I would come home with a nice bottle, strangely-named, that my kind publican knew would do for the occasion.

But embarrassing moments like these are now a thing of the past, thanks to my late-in-life experience of a wine-tasting.

After a day of sipping, I discovered two things. First, one should never taste wine on an empty stomach. Second, I am a 'Semillon Blanc' kind of girl. Proud and informed, I now walk confidently into my local off licence and calmly ask for "a really, *really* good Semillon Blanc… for under £10.00!"

Many could argue the merits of a good Merlot over a Pinot Noir, but at the end of the day it is just a matter of taste and opinion. I like Semillon Blanc. That's the choice for me. My son loves Coke – that's his choice.

Seeking God in an age of spiritual choices

What has this to do with spirituality, you may well ask?

Too many of us make the mistake of treating our spirituality in the same way as a wine-tasting, or the search for a great restaurant, or an insurance policy. The consumerism that dominates here in the Western world leads us to think that, just like selecting the right wine, I can choose the right spirituality for me. All the choices are equally good – the best one simply a matter of opinion. And there are a lot of choices out there!

Our culture considers spirituality merely a matter of taste and suitability, as if we were browsing in a supermarket of spiritual choices. A bit of Hindu, a bit of tarot, a bit of superstition, a bit of Christian morality, a bit of what feels right… and there you have it! "My spiritual life is what will help *me* live with *myself* and the decisions *I* make, what helps *me* achieve inner contentment, what helps *me* discover *my* place in the cosmos…"

As a result, we become our own authority on interpreting life and determining truth. Yet surely there is a certain foolishness in making *ourselves* – our own needs and desires – the criteria for discovering 'God'. Are we really cut out to tackle the eternal alone? Because our needs and perceptions change, does this mean our 'god' changes with them? Have we really discovered God, or is he/she really just fashioned in our image, packaged in a 'me-sized box' that suits us? Is a spirituality like this really able to help in this life or beyond?

If we are truly honest, this is not seeking God. It is *being* God. Those of you who just want to play in the market place and seek only that which serves *'me'* would be well-advised to skip the rest of this chapter. But if you want to discover the *real* God – to find *true* spirituality in the bustling marketplace of choices – then I urge you to read on.

Here is the vital question that begs to be answered: *how do we seek the real God – be there one, or many, or none – in an age of spiritual choices?*

Will the real God please stand up?

Those seeking God in an age of spiritual choices must clearly understand that most of these choices actually say many conflicting things. We are often lulled into believing that all religions are basically the same and lead to the same end. However, this is far from the truth, even by their own definitions!

Our first problem in finding the real God is our current politically correct climate. Our society persists in upholding tolerance as our highest value. Dare anyone call one belief more valid or true than another? By seeking the real God, we risk the awkward and 'intolerable' situation where we have to declare one more superior than another.

I think we desire to accept all beliefs as equal and valid for two reasons.

We do so, firstly, *because we want peace.*

In an age of terrorism, we fear that religious conviction will lead to religious intolerance, discrimination or violence. The number of wars in the world ostensibly fuelled by religion – to say nothing of the wars over the family table and in the pub – are enough for people to demand that all beliefs are good and valid in the hope that this will promote peace.

This is a fair and noble creed, but is unworkable in practical terms. Even on the family level, let alone a community and world level, we want to affirm the health of a place that allows room for disagreement, differing opinions and strong convictions to which not all need hold. This is a place that treats individuals with acceptance without insisting on agreement; a place that encourages understanding and debate rather than ignorant tolerance; a place where unity does not mean uniformity. A home which does not allow for disagreement or varying points of view is a dangerous place to be. How much more so a community.

We are pressured to accept 'pub wisdom' – never talk politics and religion! We think that by accepting all religions as true and correct we are being tolerant and this will promote peace. This is not true tolerance at all, and will not produce lasting peace.

True tolerance and the 'peace' which results is not my naïve willingness to accept the position of another as right and true. On the contrary, it is the more admirable ability to treat with respect a person with whom I have dialogue but deeply disagree. A tolerant Muslim is not someone who accepts the Buddhist doctrine of birth and rebirth – an intolerable belief for a Muslim. Rather, it is someone who rejects such a teaching while remaining respectful and compassionate towards Buddhists themselves.

A truly tolerant person can strongly disagree with another and argue her position, but will defend wholeheartedly that person's right to her different opinion and belief without fear of persecution, suppression or ridicule. This has been the basis of the more enduring 'peace' in mixed religious communities over the centuries.

Ironically, the danger with the kind of 'tolerance' that accepts all beliefs as equal and true is that it so easily leads to prejudice, violence and suspicion because we haven't bothered to find out what people really believe. We are prone to assume they are 'all the same'. When we observe something like the horror of July 11, suddenly the world thinks 'all Muslims are terrorists' because in our ignorance and 'acceptance' we haven't bothered to find out what true Islamic belief is.

We must understand true tolerance. We must be free to contradict, but never to disrespect; free to persuade, but never to coerce; free to engage and discuss rather than be fearful, hostile or ignorant.

If we all operated on that level, then the pub would have room for politics and religion, and we would be far more enlightened as a result.

This leads us to the second reason we desire to see all beliefs as equal and valid. *It is easier that way.*

Our generation is prone to seeking the easiest path for many and varied reasons. *"The road less travelled is less travelled for a reason"* says comedian Jerry Seinfeld. We have become a culture that doesn't think: where discussion and debate are not valued; where we want answers handed to us on a plate; where we desire instant gratification and instant solutions. We are often too lazy, too busy or too stressed to do the hard work of entering into the world of someone who thinks and believes differently from us and finding out what they are on about. It is far easier to say "Good on you", or "Whatever, it's all the same anyway…" and remain ignorant.

To seek God in an age of spiritual choices, we must come to terms with just how contradictory those choices are. We need to make it very clear that most of these choices say many conflicting things.

Will the real God please stand up and be counted?

An excerpt from a poem by Steve Turner describes our current religious/political climate well:

> *We believe in Marxfreudanddarwin*
> *We believe everything is OK*
> *as long as you don't hurt anyone,*
> *to the best of your definition of hurt,*
> *and to the best of your knowledge.*
>
> *We believe that all religions are basically the same—*
> *at least the one that we read was.*
> *They all believe in love and goodness.*
> *They only differ on matters of*
> *creation, sin, heaven, hell, God, and salvation.*[1]

Many religions and spiritual practices are similar in that they seek to answer the same big questions of life. Is there an afterlife? What is the purpose of my life? Will I be held accountable for my life? How can I make up for my mistakes? Is there forgiveness? Does what I do, and who I am, really matter anyway?

Yet most spiritualities and religions on offer have incredibly different answers to such questions.

Take, for example, what followers of the Eastern religions of Hinduism, Sikhism and Buddhism believe regarding the question of what is God like:

- Classical Hinduism – a vast array of gods.
- Classical Sikhism – just one deity who alone is worthy of worship.
- Classical Buddhism – no gods at all.

Contradictions? Plenty! If there are many gods there cannot possibly be just one. If there is only one god there cannot possibly be many. If there are no gods at all, then there cannot be many or just one.

All three should respect each other's humanity and freedom of expression, but we cannot ask them (unless they throw their brains out!) to regard each other's understanding of god as all equally true.

Likewise, to say to a Muslim that she is to accept Hinduism as equally true and correct would be deeply offensive. The fundamental Muslim belief that God is One and there are no other gods is in complete conflict to the Hindu belief that God is many. One cannot accept such opposing beliefs as being both true! God cannot be only one but also many at the same time.

I have criticised our Western culture for not thinking too hard. Yet to decide on our own who represents the true God would involve more lifetimes than we have. There is a need for a lifetime of research to determine what is on offer, and then a lifetime of experience to give each religion a go and see how it delivers. I don't have the time or the lifetimes! So where does one start?

Will the real God please stand up and give us some clues?

We do have clues.

Any impartial observer of our world recognises that it screams of a Designer – from the subatomic to the miraculous complexity of our own bodies, to the vast expanses of the universe. However, we may conclude that this Being is, at the same time, both wonderful (seen in the birth of a child, a beautiful sunset, or an unfolding flower) and terrible (seen in the devastation of a tsunami, the suffering of a cancer victim or the horror of war). If the question, "Is there a God?" is partly answered, another more vital question is raised: "Is this God knowable?"

Another clue is our own humanity. We have the unique human attribute of conscience, all cultures having a deep sense of knowing right from wrong. We have the ability to love, to be artistic, to yearn for meaning – all God-given characteristics. Yet that still doesn't fill in the blanks. I would suggest that we could never find God unless he chose to *reveal* himself to us first. Let me explain why.

I have been enamoured since my teenage years with the singer/songwriter James Taylor. My family – non-worshippers of James – are long-suffering. My running commentary on every song, its meaning and its timing in James' life accompanies his music whenever it is played. As *Carolina In My Mind* begins, I wax lyrical that the song was about his misery in boarding school and desire to come home. When he croons out *That's Why I'm Here*, I remind those present that he wrote it after two decades of booze and drug addiction had been finally kicked. I reminisce like we are old friends. What are my sources?

My clues? Collected interviews with his ex-wife, newspaper reports, DVD's and TV documentaries. I had the man summed up.

So I was nothing short of elated when I was given two tickets to see him in concert, which I attended with my hesitant husband. After a wonderful concert, numerous commentaries by myself and a suitably impressed hubby, I walked to the stage door to meet the man himself. You see, the tickets came with the condition that I had to come home with a photo of James! After 20 minutes, out he came. I walked confidently to the man I knew so well, ready for a photo together. As he smiled politely for the many cameras and autograph hunters, he then turned and asked for my name!

The reality hit. I was a stranger to him. Our worlds had never really touched. Despite my incredible amount of information *about him* – some true, much not – it was not the same as *knowing him*… I realised I would only know the true James Taylor if I asked him out for coffee and he chose to reveal all of himself to me in a true and honest way. He declined. So, despite my reliable sources, he would continue to be a stranger, and I remain a distant admirer, not a personal friend.

The point is that if we are to know the true God, He has to make himself known. Apart from Him coming to us and revealing himself, it will always be guesswork.

Will the real God please stand up and make a personal appointment?

The unique claim of the Christian faith lies in this very issue. The founder, Jesus of Nazareth, claimed to be God visiting this planet.

Jesus is often portrayed as a man running down blossoming meadows in a flowing kaftan with flowers around his neck, bringing love and goodwill to all mankind. No-one has a problem with such an image, surely? Yet at 33 years of age he was executed. Not so much for anything he did, but for who he claimed to be.

The truth is, though historians and people of the day (followers and opponents alike) would say he was an exemplary human being of amazing love and compassion, he was also radically controversial. The religious establishment often called him demon-possessed. His own family members thought him mad at times. His closest followers were sometimes confused.

Consider this claim:

> "Do not believe me unless I do what my Father does. But if I do it, even though you do not believe me, believe the miracles, that you may know and understand that the Father is in me, and I in the Father." Again they tried to seize him, but he escaped their grasp. [2]

His accusers were frothing at the mouth about this incredible claim of his own divinity.

Anyone can make an outrageous claim. It is only those who produce proof that we listen to. I have had many occasions to meet people who claimed they were God. Most end up institutionalised! But what if one made that claim and then pulled off the miraculous – did the impossible? What if they healed the sick, made the lame walk and the blind see? What if they spoke tenderly to deep pain no-one else knew about, and offered forgiveness to the burdened and hope to the downcast? These are things only God can do. This is what Jesus did.

If you want to know what God is like, Jesus says, then listen to my words. Then, if that isn't enough, look at what I do. He stands in a league of his own as a spiritual leader. All other spiritual leaders point the way to God, enlighten the path to God, suggest the practices that will draw you closer to God. Jesus of Nazareth proclaimed himself as God's visual expression! God's personal visit! No wonder they killed him – it was an outrageous claim!

Jesus' life and his death make any other conclusions impossible. He worked miracles, he calmed storms, he delivered the demon-possessed with the authority of a more powerful being. Jesus had inexplicable knowledge of life and the afterlife, saying he would allow his life to be taken and then rise from the dead (as if he had the power to determine life and death, and to overcome death). He then backed this up with the original Easter experience.

Will the real God please find me?

Where do I start seeking?

Start first with the one who said:

> "*I and the Father are one. If you know me, you will know the Father*".[3]

Start with the one who declared:

> "*I am the light of the world. Whoever follows me will never walk in darkness, but will have the light of life*".[4]

Jesus revealed God's mind and heart to us and called people to respond with all their heart, mind, soul and strength:

> "*If anyone loves me, he will obey my teaching. My Father will love him, and we will come to him and make our home with him*".[5]

If seeking God in an age of spiritual choices, start with Jesus.

ENDNOTES

1. Steve Turner (English Journalist), *Creed*, his satirical poem on the modern mind
2. John 10:37   3. John 10:30   4. John 8:12   5. John 14:23

Contentment
Wendy Potts

What is it with us and those lifestyle shows? We can't seem to get enough of them.

We're a generation enlightened by the ideals of *Ground Force, House Doctor* and *Ready, Steady, Cook*. We are culturally savvy. We know that roasted meat should be 'rested', that 'texture is the new colour' and (my personal favourite) that the lives of ordinary families can be transformed in just one weekend when an entire house and garden is renovated, bringing real unity and untold joy.

But just stop and imagine for a moment how the circulation would plummet if *Better Homes* became a rather shorter magazine called *Perfectly Adequate Homes*…

Or if on a new five minute version of *House Doctor* Anne Maurice says:

> *"As you can see, the Potts family home has plenty of potential.*
> *We could do loads with this one.*
> *However, it does the job pretty well.*
> *It's warm and dry and comfortable.*
> *No obvious structural problems.*
> *We're going to encourage the Potts to be content and leave it as it is."* (Cut to closing credits)[1]

We're not good at contentment are we?

The reason this show would seem ridiculous is that most of us have accepted the assumption these lifestyle programmes are built on: that is, life will be richer, fuller and happier when we raise our standard of living by putting in a water feature or giving our kitchen a makeover.

Don't get me wrong – I am right there in the target market: middle income, middle-aged with three young children. I am a designer with a love of colour and beautiful things and my home is an expression of that (if you can ignore the peanut butter smeared on the sofa). The thought of wandering through IKEA for half an hour on my own is very appealing.

But my own experience is that the buzz from 'retail therapy' and 'renovation therapy' is very short-lived. As much fun as it is, it doesn't ultimately deliver lasting contentment. There will always be the next thing I think I need. It's not a great long-term solution for completeness. We already enjoy one of the highest standards of living in the world. So if contentment in life is about getting more stuff, don't you think we should have 'arrived'?

The more you eat, the emptier you get

I'm not alone. A recent newspaper report discussed some interesting research done recently on the relationship between wealth and happiness. The findings show that despite the fact that we have never been richer (a real income three times higher than in the 1950's), we are still chronically discontent:

> "We may be better off in the sense that we own more stuff, but that doesn't seem to make us any happier... A key explanation suggested by the psychologists is the speed with which our expectations and aspirations adjust to changed

circumstances... What at first was new and wonderful soon becomes what we're used to and have come to expect. Thus do yesterday's luxuries become today's necessities."[2]

It's worth listening to those who've 'had it all'. Of course, not all would agree, but some, like actor Mel Gibson, say having everything is not all it's cracked up to be:

"Let's face it; I've been to the pinnacle of what secular utopia has to offer. It's just this kind of everything. I've got money, fame, this that and the other, you know, and it's all been like, whoosh, here you go. And it's okay. And when I was younger, I got my proboscis out and I dipped it in the font and sucked it up, all right. It didn't matter, there wasn't enough, it wasn't good enough. It's not good enough. It leaves you empty. The more you eat, the emptier you get."[3]

We know there's more to life than accumulating things. Our experience tells us that the most important things in life are not found packaged on a shelf. Sometimes we get just a glimpse of what really counts – a jolting reminder that the fundamental things cannot be bought with money.

Recently, some old friends told us that their 14-year-old son, who was born with Cystic Fybrosis, has six months to live. Getting that new sofa suddenly doesn't rate so highly anymore.

Jesus' unsettling words

It seems that materialism isn't just a modern disease. Jesus said something about the subject to his hearers two thousand years ago.

There is something unsettling about how relevant his words are to us now:

> *"Take care. Protect yourself against the least bit of greed.*
> *Owning a lot of things won't make your life safe."*[4]

His words resonate with a strong warning of spiritual danger. He does not treat the issue lightly at all. He goes on to tell a story about a man who had it all in the eyes of those around him, but not so in the eyes of God. It speaks to our generation every bit as powerfully as it did to his.

And he told them this parable:

"The ground of a certain rich man produced a good crop. He thought to himself, 'What shall I do? I have no place to store my crops.'

"Then he said, 'This is what I'll do. I will tear down my barns and build bigger ones, and there I will store all my grain and my goods. And I'll say to myself, "You have plenty of good things laid up for many years. Take life easy; eat, drink and be happy."'

"But God said to him, 'You fool! This very night your life will be demanded from you. Then who will get what you have prepared for yourself?'

"This is how it will be with anyone who stores up things for themselves but is not rich toward God."[5]

It's a story with a sting in the tail. This man believes that his wealth will bring him happiness. He believes he has it all sewn up. At least he will have, just around the corner – after some necessary renovations. Then he'll kick back and enjoy himself. He'll have everything he needs in life. But this is very different from the way God sees it.

The point of Jesus' story is that this man had made some seriously foolish oversights. Despite appearances, he had not invested wisely at all. His first mistake was…

Living as if wealth would bring security

The problem is that wealth is deceptively fragile. Just think of the blue chip companies which have crashed in the last decade – Enron, Equitable Life, Onetel…

One of the most scandalous events in the financial world was undoubtedly the single-handed destruction of Britain's ancient Barings bank by a 28-year-old trader, Nicholas Leeson. He lost more than a billion dollars in high-risk trades on Japan's Nikkei exchange in 1995. I get stressed just losing my wallet.

Not only is wealth fragile, but life itself is fragile. Death is not really in our control at all. Just suspend reality for a moment and imagine the day that Death comes knocking…

"Hi I'm looking for Wendy Potts."

"Hi, I'm Wendy. What can I do for you?"

"Actually I'm here to do something for you. Your name has just come up. It's time for you to die."

"Oh … This is not a good time really. I'm just in the middle of making school lunches – I'm in a bit of a rush actually. We're running late. Can you call back later?

A better time…? Ummm… no tomorrow's not really good for me either – I've got a deadline for that piece I'm writing and then it's the football presentation in the evening… Next week's pretty impossible. We've got visitors coming to stay…"

As if we could tell death not to turn up!

We tend to live as if we'll never die. It's just too hard to imagine not being here. But we are foolish not to consider it. The statistics are pretty convincing – it will be our turn one day. We would be wise to be prepared. The rich farmer was judged a fool because he was short-sighted. He prepared too well for this life but was totally unprepared for his death.

One of the traps of materialism is that it blinds us to the possibility that life is more than what is here and now. Jesus teaches that we are eternal beings, made for an eternity with God (or an eternity without him if we choose). He makes clear that this life is just a small speck on the scale of eternity. Why should we be convinced he is right? Let me suggest two reasons:

1. Our experience tells us

Everything in us cries out that there must be more... Maybe it's camping under the stars that does it for you – that vast unending universe which reminds us just how small we are. It could be the birth of your child – the miracle of new life within – that speaks volumes about a Designer that is way beyond ourselves. Or perhaps the death of someone you love grips you with a deep sense that there must be more.

When a baby is in the womb, it cannot have any comprehension of what lies beyond the walls of its small universe. What if, like babies, we are just on the edge of something so much bigger, something just around the corner and out of sight, but very real?

2. Jesus' experience tells us

Jesus died and then rose to life three days later. That experience lends credibility to his claims about life and eternity. Whatever theories we may have need to be weighed against Jesus' words. Why? Beating death puts him in a league of his own. His words are worth trusting when it comes to eternity. What's more, to all those who trust him he offers certainty about life after death.

Not only did the rich farmer live in denial of death, he lived in denial of God. His second and biggest mistake was...

Living as if God didn't exist

He had no recognition that his life and wealth came from God. He lived as if he was completely independent from his Maker. We don't know much about this guy, whether he was morally upright or a bit dodgy; whether he treated his employees with fairness or ripped them off; whether he cheated on his wife or was a model husband. All Jesus tells us is that he was not *"rich towards God."* That's what tipped the balance for him.

So what does that mean?

If you'd asked this guy on the street "Do you believe in God?" he might have answered "yes", but in his day to day life he went on as if God wasn't there.

Listen again to the man in the story. It's all about him: "*My* crops, *my* barns, *my* grain, *my* goods…" He depended on God for the rain and the sunshine, but there was no room in his thinking for God who made his crops grow. He consulted himself about the decisions he made without reference to God. He was at the centre of his own life. God didn't rate a look in.

Isn't that what we are all like most of the time? It's an easy mistake to make.

That was me once. I believed God existed. I just lived as if he didn't. I didn't want him to be 'God' in my life. I certainly didn't want him to tell me how to live and spoil my fun, so I made sure he stayed at a polite distance.

Failing to be rich towards God

I think one of the reasons we like to avoid God is because we think of him as a kill-joy who will limit our freedom. The rich man's mistake was *not* that he enjoyed the good things he had. The Bible's view is that the opposite is true. God is the *Designer* of the good things. He has been incredibly 'rich towards us'. He has given us good things for our pleasure. It's not a mistake to enjoy the physical world.

The rich man's mistake was living in God's world as if God wasn't there. He was not 'rich towards God' who had been so rich towards him. He had no relationship with the Giver.

Wouldn't you find that highly offensive? God does.

The Bible tells us we are unique creatures – lovingly made by God for a friendship with him. What an incredible concept – a friendship with the Creator of the Universe! What a privilege! But when we ignore God and look to the created things of this world to fulfill us instead of the Creator, he is rightly offended and we, who are made for so much more, are left unfulfilled.

As a race we are 'out of sync' with God. The Bible says this is the reason our world is in such a mess. Death and decay and discontent are just symptoms of that.

Augustine, a famous sceptic who avoided God for many years and then finally gave in, said these words: *"You have made us for yourself, Lord. Our hearts are restless until they find their rest in you."*

Finding true contentment

Perhaps you recognise this restlessness in your own heart. That restlessness can be a blessing in disguise if it leads you to God. You see, the best this world has to offer is hollow and empty in the end if not enjoyed in the company of the Giver.

So what does it mean to be rich towards God? It's simply living life as we were designed to – in a rich relationship with him. It's about letting him fill and influence your world. Giving him the central place he deserves in our lives. Nothing else will satisfy the human heart.

Christianity is all about the God who generously pursues this relationship with us.

The message of Christianity is that although we have pushed God to one side, he has not abandoned us. Instead he sends his own Son, who by his death, pays the price for our offence against God and invites us back into relationship with him, now and for eternity.

The difference this makes is enormous. This means I can enjoy the best of this world without clinging too tightly to it, because my security is found in a relationship with my Maker instead of the things he has made. He helps me to hold them lightly and share them more generously.

This means I can face the worst of this world without despair because I know this is not as good as it gets. My real home is yet to come.

This means I can face death itself without denial or fear, because I know the one who will bring me through is trustworthy. My ultimate security is found in him.

Jesus' story calls each of us to stop and take stock of our lives:

Am I in danger of making the same mistakes as the rich farmer?

Have I been investing my life in the things that last or that which is temporary?

Do I have a rich relationship with God or do I live as if he doesn't exist?

Have I been looking for contentment in places that can't deliver?

ENDNOTES
1. Adapted with permission from Tony Payne's article 'The Secret of Contentment', *The Briefing*, Issue 282
2. Ross Gittens, *The Sydney Morning Herald*, 4 September 2002
3. *Sixty Minutes* 22.02.04, 'The Passion Interview Transcript', Reporter: Diane Sawyer, Producer: Primetime
4. Luke 12:15 (Contemporary English Version)
5. Luke 12:16-21

Stability
Red Fulton

*W*hen was the last time you made a change?

I remember a TV commercial featuring a woman in a doctor's surgery waiting for her appointment. She looks around and considers how the room might look better if it were redecorated. In a flash, she is out of her chair – ripping up the carpet, moving furniture around and fixing the blinds. Her doctor calls her name and as she looks around at the newly decorated room, she declares, "Oh, it's OK now, I feel much better!"

Apparently her renovation is therapeutic – it is just what she's needed! The advertisers then tell us to buy from their homeware shop, and we'll feel much better too. It's clever advertising because they have tapped into something that women find appealing.

Renovating more than the house

We love to renovate, redecorate and revamp – and I'm not just talking about our bedrooms or our homes. I'm talking about ourselves.

My wardrobe is in a constant state of being upgraded whenever the budget allows (and sometimes when it doesn't). We change our hair colour, our lip gloss, our diets, our hobbies and our careers fairly regularly, and they are just the small changes! Sometimes women change their partners (once the novelty wears off) or their morals (if they interfere with their lifestyle).

After all, another change is as good as a holiday. Or is it?

This largely female trend indicates that women are creatures who *love* change, who thrive on flexibility, and embrace uncertainty. Does that sound like you?

In fact, a newspaper ran an article recently declaring that there was a new breed of woman in town – the 'contrasexual'. She is in her late 20's/early 30's, very confident, self-sufficient, strategic, business-minded, and sees sex as recreational rather than emotional. She is not looking for anything which might lock her into commitment or stability. This woman is apparently no longer interested in searching for anything permanent but has taken control of her own destiny and purposefully flits from one change to the next. She has moved on from desiring contentment in such stale areas as home/husband/heirs.

Perhaps, though, if we take a deeper look at our own motives for change, we might discover that we are not as different from our mothers and grandmothers as these recent reports suggest.

Searching for stability

What is it that drives our decisions to make another change?

Could it be that we keep changing things in our lives because we are *frantically searching for something permanent*? We fumble from one change to the next, trying to find something stable and solid – something which will satisfy for more than a month. Every time we think we've found the ideal thing to keep us grounded and content, we discover yet again that it is just a mirage. The reality is not like the dream and so off we go to continue our search elsewhere. *Could our obsession with change actually be a desperate search for stability?*

This quote by Jesus Christ explains exactly what we are longing for and reveals how we can get our hands on it.

"Everyone who hears these words of mine and puts them into practice is like a wise man who built his house on the rock. The rain came down, the streams rose, and the winds blew and beat against that house; yet it did not fall, because it had its foundation on the rock. But everyone who hears these words of mine and does not put them into practice is like a foolish man who built his house on sand. The rain came down, the streams rose, and the winds blew and beat against that house, and it fell with a great crash."[1]

It's not a story about how to find a good builder, is it? Yet it hits the nail right on the head because we all know that sinking feeling… that feeling in the pit of your stomach when something in your life, which you thought was firm, has given way or been pulled out from under your feet… A drowning kind of feeling that, once experienced, we try desperately to avoid.

These are the experiences Jesus *wants* us to avoid. He has seen the devastation caused when people build their lives on things that are fragile. The point he made so clearly to his original audience over two thousand years ago still grips us today with its striking relevance to our own lives.

Did you pick up his main point? **What you build your life on really matters.**

Let me put it another way. If your foundation is movable, says Jesus, then you are a disaster waiting to happen.

So often we make the mistake of building our lives on all sorts of sand masquerading as rock. In the area where I live, there is some land which cannot be built on because it falls within the boundaries of what is known as a 100-year-flood area. To the naked eye, the land looks good – solid, perfect for development. Yet history tells us that it regularly goes underwater. Knowing this fact ought to make people reconsider their building plans. The building of our lives can be just as hazardous and so Jesus' warning and promise are well worth investigating.

True stories

Recently, I spoke to a number of women who have become Christians and I asked them what they used to build their lives on before taking to heart these words of Jesus. Their responses were typical of many women today.

(A) *Name:* Jennifer.

Took Jesus' words to heart: 18 months ago.

Previous foundation: Money. She explained that she and her husband spent their time thinking about how they could make more money or win more money or scam more money. Not out of greed but because they thought money would be a good foundation for them and their children. They thought it would bring security and freedom.

Jesus' view: Money is just sand masquerading as rock!

(B) *Name:* Helen

Took Jesus' words to heart: 30 years ago.

Previous foundation: Family happiness. All her effort was put into looking after her husband and setting up a happy peaceful environment for her three small children. Her own purpose and happiness was entirely tied up in them. They were her motivation and inspiration. Her husband came home one day and announced that he no longer loved her enough to continue the marriage and would be immediately moving in with his secretary (who apparently no longer loved her husband enough to stay with him either).

Jesus' view: Family happiness is just sand masquerading as rock!

True stability

I spoke recently with a single young woman who had never really recovered from her mother's sudden death 12 years ago.

She wasn't familiar with this part of the Bible, but as we discussed why her mum's death was still so personally crushing for her, she looked at me – her face still smeared with the pain of grief – and said "She was my rock – and now she's gone."

It's a terrible feeling when something we imagined or hoped would last forever is lost or ripped out from under our feet. These kinds of experiences can leave us reeling for years. The reality of death means that even our closest relationships are sand masquerading as rock.

It is true that if you build your life on Jesus and his words you will still face the 'storms of life' such as suffering, loneliness, relationship breakdown, unemployment and sickness. However, the extraordinary thing for the woman who trusts and follows Christ is that her rock remains unmoved. It is eternal. Even during the terrible darkness of grief over others or when faced with her own death – the woman who has reached out for the rock and taken Jesus' words to heart has a foundation which is solid. It cannot be stolen, broken, removed or ruined in any way.

Just stop and think about that for a moment. Our foundation doesn't change, leave, or die. *Do you long for that kind of stability?*

Look at Jesus' words again… Did you notice how Jesus describes the person who builds on the rock? He says it is the one who "hears my words *and puts them into practice*".

That's something I love about Jesus – he really hates hypocrisy. He wants us to listen to him *and* obey him. He says there are only two categories of people: wise and foolish. Wise people follow Jesus' words and foolish people don't. Sounds a bit arrogant, don't you think? Unless, of course, Jesus is actually God in the flesh. He is our maker, our designer. He knew you before you were born and it was he who knitted you together in your mother's womb. He knows you intimately and loves you deeply, and it is God's desire to direct your life towards himself – the one solid rock. When we consider who

Jesus is, it is really no surprise that he knows how we ought to live. He offers wisdom, security and hope. Sadly, not everyone accepts what he so generously offers.

How stable is your rock?

I'm 8 months pregnant as I write this. Obviously, I see changes taking place every time I look in the mirror – some beautiful, some horrifying! Personally, one of the changes I really enjoy during pregnancy is that my bra size increases dramatically. Right now I'm wearing a 38D and I love it! I even pause a bit longer when purchasing a bra in the hope that someone might see me buying my new and impressive size. Unfortunately, these two amazing additions to my chest are temporary. There is *nothing permanent about them*. This time next year they will not only have shrunk, they will be a number of inches closer to the floor.

Why am I telling you this? Because money, success, romance and family are all good things given to us by God for our enjoyment (just like my breasts), but I want to urge you not to think of these good gifts as your *rock*. There is nothing permanent about them. When it comes to building your life, make Jesus your solid foundation and he will help you to stand firm through the storms of life.

Some of you are willing to admit, *"I'm tired of stumbling around in shifting sand. I want a rock that is immovable."*

If this is you, then God has officially declared you a *renovator's dream*! Jesus is ready to begin work straight away.

> *Trust in the Lord forever, for the Lord God is an everlasting rock.*[2]

ENDNOTES
1. Matthew 7:24-27
2. Isaiah 26:4 (English Standard Version)

Christine's **story**

I think I am the worst person I have ever known. Before I became a Christian, I was totally self-centred and intent on seeking happiness at anybody and everybody else's expense. If there was anybody God should have written off, it was me. But that's not what he did. Let me tell you about it…

I was born the eldest of three kids. Ours was a close family, doing crazy things like camping on the beach while Dad fished and Mum read books. Mum was a school teacher and I thought the sun shone out of her. But like every kid there was a rebellious streak in me. I can remember when I was about 11 a lady from the area came to our house and asked if I wanted to go to church. The way she asked made it sound as if Mum wouldn't let me, but Mum just said, "Ask her." So of course I said yes!

But once I got there, I soon realised it wasn't naughty, just meaningless. We sing-song chanted a whole lot of words and I didn't have a clue what I was saying. But they told me I was a Christian, just for being there. So I believed them.

When I was 14, I started going out with Dominic, a young Italian Roman Catholic boy. It was in this time of my adolescence that I realised how satisfying a sexual relationship was to me, and what impact that would have on the rest of my life. I began sleeping with Dominic when I was 15, and we finally married when I was 20.

Our marriage was OK for a few years. I was very busy

with three young kids and Dominic was a workaholic, and our relationship had to fit in around these constraints. But as the kids got older, I became more restless. Dominic was often away for long periods with work, and I went looking elsewhere to satisfy my cravings.

Somehow I had picked up this weird idea that God loved Catholics and not Protestants. Therefore he didn't love me. I had made sure that the kids were baptised as Catholics, so that at least he would love them! If God didn't love me, then maybe other men would.

Or maybe I could *become* a good Catholic. I enrolled to do some lessons with the nun at the RC church. But on the night I turned up for my first lesson, she apologised that she had been called out on an emergency. Having a spare night of freedom on my hands, I spent it at the pub, and then lied to Dominic about where I had been. After that I found it easy to spin a web of lies to cover my tracks. And the tracks weren't pretty. They involved bouts of heavy drinking and sexual encounters with different men.

It was at one of these nights at the pub that I met Richard – a charming, sophisticated smooth business man. It wasn't long before I had moved in with him. I was so self-centred that I was prepared to leave my husband *and* three primary-school-aged children in order to satisfy my own desires. Not only did I leave them, but I didn't want a family life either. I told myself this was real love this time.

Richard was quite a womaniser before I moved in with him, and somehow I expected that to stop. We lived together for 6 years, and then got married. I was desperate to marry him, because as far as I was concerned, that meant we belonged to each other. Richard would have to be faithful to me now.

We moved to North, made lots of money, and seemed happy. We embraced the New Age lifestyle of crystals, massages and aromatherapy. But I didn't see what was happening under my very nose – Richard was having an affair with my secretary. So I took off back home. If he was going to be unfaithful, I'd find ways of enjoying myself, too.

This was probably the blackest period of my life. At the time I thought I was living the high life, but it was filled with sordid weekends, nightclubs, nights in hotel rooms, men whose names I can't even remember. To recall it now fills me with such shame, but you need to know that's who I was. It makes what God did all the more amazing…

One night while I was a racecourse with a group of friends, I met Brian. He was a horse-trainer, a gentle sort of guy. I delighted in saying and doing things which were meant to shock him. But he just looked sad. I wasn't really attracted to him – he was several years younger than me – but because I had no-one else better on the line at the time, Brian and I moved in together. I soon discovered that Brian came from a Christian family and knew about Christ, but wanted to live life his own way.

Probably the beginning of my encounter with God was the impending wedding of my daughter. She had rung and said that she wanted the wedding party and immediate family to take communion during the wedding service. I readily agreed, but Brian was concerned and said I couldn't possibly do it because I wasn't a Christian. I wanted to prove he was wrong and decided to go back to church and 'bone up' on taking communion.

But where would I go? A couple of months before, Brian and I had gone to a local church for the baptism of the children of one of his friends. I remember being quite taken aback. It was nothing like the churches I had gone to before. People were overwhelmingly friendly, and there were none of those meaningless chants! I'd gone again a few times after the baptism, but only when it was raining on a Sunday and I couldn't play tennis.

But now I was going to go regularly, just to prove Brian wrong and show him I *was* a Christian and could take communion. I went, and by the time the wedding came around, I didn't think there was anything to stop me taking communion. I may have been more promiscuous than the other women I met at church, but I was still basically OK.

About six weeks after my daughter's wedding, my world fell apart. My mother, whom I adored beyond belief, dropped dead with an aneurism in the middle of a concert. This intelligent woman was not meant to die so young. Questions and thoughts crowded in on me. I realised my world was really very empty, and now it was emptier than ever. What *was* life all about? What was I doing living with this bloke? I had no commitment to him, but I couldn't give him up. Now that Mum had died, I needed someone – someone to cling to, someone to hold me. I felt so guilty that I was just using him, but I couldn't stop.

I also felt driven to keep going to church. Someone there picked up that I was uneasy about things, and asked if I would like to do a short course which investigated Christianity and answered any questions I might have about the Christian faith. I figured I had done lots of self-help courses before, so one more wouldn't hurt.

But this course was different. It certainly wasn't self-help! It was more like a brain-explosion. I realised how destitute I was before God, what a mess I'd made of my life and that I was in big trouble if I kept on rejecting God like I had. Sure, I'd had a 'good time', and I was motoring ahead in my business, but *there was nothing in it*. The emperor had no clothes! It was as if God was saying to me, "Chris, stop side-stepping me and listen to me. I've got more for you than this. But you have to do it my way."

I felt stuck. I certainly couldn't go back because I realised that would be running away from God. But I didn't think I could go forward either. I thought that if I gave in and committed myself to God, that I would have to give up everything I'd ever known. Specifically, I'd never be able to sleep with another man again! Eventually, I concluded that if that was the cost, so be it. So, in my living room on a Wednesday afternoon in March, 1993, I said, "OK, God. I'll give it up. I'll do it your way."

I certainly wasn't prepared for what was to come. First, there was the release from the guilt of the past. While I was in it, my mind had become dulled to the selfishness of using people for my own satisfaction, but now I was overcome with the enormity of it all. It wasn't only the way I'd treated people, but also the way I'd treated God. But God assured me that he'd forgiven me. And it was Jesus' death that was the key to forgiveness. It proved to me that God was serious about his desire to establish a new relationship with me. It blew me away that God was willing to put his son through the pain of the crucifixion for me.

Secondly, the new world God opened up for me was infinitely better than the life I'd given up. There were new friends, new plans, new fun things to do. It was like all my Christmases had come at once. I can honestly say that I didn't miss the drinking, the nightclubs, the poker machines… I looked back on the past 45 years and thought "What a waste!" I had been worried that my old life would beckon me back, but I discovered that it had no power at all. God had completely changed me, I was a new person. The Bible says, "*If anyone is in Christ, he (or she) is a new creation; the old has gone, the new has come.*"[1]

I had told Brian that first night that this was the end – I could no longer live with him. We weren't married, I thought I had just been using him, and he didn't have the same commitment to God that I had. However, God was still working in Brian's life. We stopped living together, and soon after, through the kindness of God, Brian became a Christian, too. Then he asked me to marry him.

I've been a Christian now for almost 12 years. Sometimes I stop and ask myself if it has been worth it. The answer is always a question – where else is there to go? My life before Christ was so appalling that the alternative doesn't bear thinking about. God's forgiveness of the mess I had created has given me new life. And for that I am completely in his debt. As I explained at the beginning of my story, God should have wiped me off but he didn't. He pursued me.

Should God wipe you off? Yes. Is he pursuing you? Yes. Stop and listen, stop and investigate. Don't run away – it's not worth it.

ENDNOTE
1. 2 Corinthians 5:17

Forgiveness

Narelle Jarrett

*K*athryn looked at me and said: "If you really knew what I am like, you'd know that God couldn't forgive me!"

I've heard words like these so many times. In fact, earlier in my life I also thought it would be impossible for God to forgive me.

Every day we work hard to convince others that we are really okay people. We work hard to reveal ourselves in ways we think will win their approval, acceptance, trust, friendship and even their love.

Yet we know in our hearts that we have sometimes hurt others, that we have deep regrets and certainly we don't want others to know about that time when…! We all struggle to be likeable, trustworthy, caring and fun to be with.

On the whole, we have worked out life fairly satisfactorily, and most of us generally get by. But when we stop and think about our real selves – the hidden self that only we truly know – we doubt that anyone who knew that other side could love us or want us or accept us. We feel wretched about many of our decisions and our careless, even reckless, attitude to others. Our regrets can be very great. But these moments of truthful reflection are usually rare. Mostly we've learned to get on, to begin again, to put things behind us, to not let the past rule the present.

Can God forgive us?

So, when would someone be likely to say: "If you really knew what I am like, you'd know that God couldn't forgive me!"?

For Kathryn, that time came as she began to explore the possibility of God's existence and to consider what the implications of that might be for her. Discovering that the God who made heaven and earth describes himself as loving and holy is very confronting. Kathryn immediately felt that God wouldn't accept her because, although in society's terms she appeared to be an upright person, she knew that in the light of God's constant love and goodness, her behaviour was full of fault. She was sure that God could neither accept her nor forgive her.

Certainly, this is how we think and operate! We don't like people who do hurtful things or who go against our standards of acceptable behaviour. In fact we pass laws to control reckless, uncaring people; we teach our children to avoid such troublemakers, and we also avoid them.

In the light of these facts, was there any hope for Kathryn? If God applied to her the same measure we use for each other, Kathryn knew she would be without hope. She felt this intensely. She was totally convinced that this God, the father of Jesus, could never love her. She felt totally lost.

The rugged journey to the truth

Like Kathryn, as we get better acquainted with God, we begin to regret our unkindness, bitterness, envy, resentment, jealousy, selfishness – the sort of things that God calls 'sin'. We remember how we have sometimes pursued life on our terms with such fervour that we've left behind us a trail of hurt people – spouse, partner, children, friends – it seems impossible to redeem the carnage we've wrought.

God's generous loving nature stands in stark contrast to our unloving, argumentative, angry selves, taking out our resentment on whoever is closest to us. "Accept me as I am!" we demand. "Too bad if I'm sometimes hard to live with – just get over it!"

It is clear why we say: "If you really knew what I am like you'd know that God couldn't forgive me!" Yet being able to acknowledge the truth about ourselves brings us a step closer to knowing the God who made us. The Lord knows already everything there is to know about us and says to us these outrageous words: I love you.

This is how he showed his love among us. He sent his one and only son into the world that we might live through him.[1]

We are astounded and confounded when we learn that God loves sinners, especially those who are aware of their failures, aware of the ways in which they have let others down, have let themselves down, and who grieve their failures.

If we claim to be without sin we deceive ourselves and the truth is not in us. If we confess our sins he is faithful and just and will forgive us our sins and take away our unrighteousness.[2]

At this point we, like Kathryn, have an important choice. We can either remain with an incomplete understanding and experience of God because we feel our case is hopeless, or we can explore the possibility that God just might be able to forgive us and help us put things to right.

God confronts us in the words in the Bible with our real nature, making it plain that no one except Jesus is able to stand before him and claim to be a wholly good and loving person. This is a rugged journey toward truthfulness. It is never easy to examine our lives in the light of such words: "You are to love the Lord your God with your whole heart, mind and body and to love your neighbour as yourself." A quick glance at our behaviour in the last week quickly reveals how we struggle to come anywhere near living lives that are characterised by love.

Yes, God confronts us, but it is a confrontation accompanied by words that promise reconciliation with God. This is because God has done everything necessary for us to be reconciled to him. All that is left to be done, we now need to do. God asks us to repent of lives lived without him and to place our trust in Jesus' death for us.

Paul's story of forgiveness

There is a story in the Bible of a man named Paul who was so angry with Jesus that he delighted in his death and pursued his friends in order to kill them. He was responsible for the murder and persecution of many Christians. He said of himself: "I persecuted the followers of Jesus to their death, arresting both men and women and throwing them into prison. I was a blasphemer and a persecutor and a violent man."

When Jesus confronted Paul, he could not pretend to be innocent. His violence was known by all. "Paul, why are you persecuting me?" Jesus asked. Confronted by Jesus himself, Paul had nowhere to hide. Terror must surely have struck his heart at that moment. How could he possibly survive God's righteous anger at his actions? Surely there could never be forgiveness!

Yet Paul later wrote:

Christ Jesus came into the world to save sinners – of whom I am the worst. But for that very reason I was

shown mercy so that in me, the worst of sinners, Christ
Jesus might display his unlimited patience as an example
to those who would believe on him and have eternal life.[3]

Here is hope for every person! Confrontation and comfort are the wonderful ways by which God brings sinners home. Paul said to a man who was struggling with his own need for forgiveness, *"Believe in the Lord Jesus and you will be saved."*[4]

Paul, the self-confessed persecutor and murderer of Christians, found acceptance with God through Jesus. Paul called himself the worst of sinners because he was so entrenched in his opposition to God's son, Jesus. Yet Paul found God merciful towards him, full of unlimited patience with him. How can this be? How could God love such a lawless, violent man? Well, it really is beyond human understanding because we just don't act like this, and therefore we do not expect God to act like this. But God is like this, and he does act like this, and it surprises us every time.

Paul discovered that his own understandings of God were wrong. So profoundly humbled was Paul by this revelation that he acknowledged his wrongful arrogance and his violent behaviour and entrusted himself completely to Jesus. Immediately, he experienced the forgiveness and acceptance of God.

Hope for Kathryn

By receiving God's mercy – by experiencing and accepting God's limitless patience – Paul became an example of hope for all people like Kathryn and me. Even if our actions were exactly like Paul's, even then there would be forgiveness. And like Paul, if we trust God to deal with us with mercy and loving patience there will be forgiveness. Whoever turns to Christ – called repenting – even though they are the worst of sinners, will experience how mercifully God will deal with them.

It is worth noting that even though we keep some sort of running register of our sins, there is truly only one sin – the rejection of Jesus and of his right to lead us in the way we live. Our wrong actions – anger, immorality, stealing, violence, murder, selfishness, envy – are symptoms of lives adrift from the God who made us and loves us.

Repentance is about changing our minds about Jesus and beginning a new life that follows his example. Paul later went on to write these words:

Be imitators of God, therefore, as dearly loved children and live a life of love, just as Christ loved us.[5]

Neither Kathryn nor I can ever say: "If you really knew what I was like you'd know that God couldn't forgive me." God shows us in Paul what a human being is capable of – violence against God and against God's friends – and he shows us the way back.

ENDNOTES
1. 1 John 3:9
2. 1 John 1:8
3. 1 Timothy 1:15-16
4. Acts 16:31
5. Ephesians 5:1

Clarity

Jennie Baddeley

What would happen if you lost your diary or the calendar where you write all the things you have to do? You'd know you were busy, but you wouldn't know why. You'd forget responsibilities, appointments, presents, bills… For most of us it would be a disaster – there is so much going on in our lives and we are too busy to keep everything in our heads. When we come to thinking about Jesus, then, we have to ask, "Does Jesus have anything relevant to say to busy women in the twenty-first century?" Can Jesus possibly understand what it is like to have such a full diary? Can he have anything to say when you have so much to do that you don't know how you are physically going to do it?

Two sisters

The surprising answer is 'yes', Jesus does have something to say. In the Bible[1], Luke records the life of Jesus and he tells us what happened when Jesus went to stay at the home of two women named Mary and Martha. He writes in his story:

> *As Jesus and his disciples were on their way, he came to a village where a woman named Martha opened her home to him. She had a sister called Mary, who sat at the Lord's feet, listening to what he said.*

Martha is shown to be enormously generous here: she invites Jesus with all his followers into her home; she prepares the food, possibly even provides beds for them. She has no washing machine, no dishwasher, no microwave – not even a fridge. She's doing it tough. Even if she has a couple of servants, it is still the kind of situation where you need everyone to help and do their bit. Mary, Martha's sister, for example, could pitch in. But where is Mary? She's not helping. She's sitting down in the lounge room with all the disciples, listening to Jesus. How does Martha react to this?

> But Martha was distracted by all the preparations that had to be made. She came to Jesus and asked, "Lord, don't you care that my sister has left me to do the work by myself? Tell her to help me!"

Choosing what's better

Martha is not happy. She is so unhappy that she interrupts the proceedings to ask Jesus a question. Does he really not care that her sister has left everything to her, or does it just *look* like he doesn't care? I don't think we're meant to see Martha as this irritated old hag who wants to boss people. Mary *is* being socially unacceptable: she's in the lounge room listening and learning, when she should be helping out in the kitchen. She should be in the kitchen helping Martha because she is Martha's sister and the family honour is at stake if they can't get all the preparations together. What Mary has chosen to do is outrageous. She's left everything to Martha and she's sitting down, doing nothing to help.

Martha's exasperation is understandable. We expect that maybe Jesus is going to tell Mary to go and pull her weight and help her sister in the kitchen. So, how does Jesus respond? Luke tells us:

> *"Martha, Martha," the Lord answered, "you are worried and upset about many things, but only one thing is needed. Mary has chosen what is better, and it will not be taken away from her."*

Jesus' response is surprising. He says that Mary is not to be sent away at all. What's more, he invites Martha to join her. He contrasts Martha with Mary:

- Here's Martha – upset and worried about many things.
- Here's Mary – she has chosen the better thing, the one thing that is needed.

In a sense, Jesus changes the question Martha asks. He *doesn't* say he doesn't care about Martha's predicament; he *does* say that Mary has chosen to listen to him and that he *cares* very much that Martha does not lose the opportunity to do the same. So Jesus doesn't tell Mary to go immediately to the kitchen and help Martha. Instead, he tells Martha that she has it wrong. She's doing many, many things; she's very busy. Nothing she is doing is wrong or bad, but she is not doing the one necessary thing. She has missed out on the one thing that is needed. Jesus says that Mary has chosen the one thing that is needed, because of *who* Mary is listening to. She is listening to Jesus.

The reason that this is so important is that Jesus was sent by God to tell us about God and to show us the way to God. That is why Jesus tells Martha that there is only one thing needed here and that Mary has chosen it. She is listening to Jesus. Listening to Jesus is more important than food, busy-ness, chores, or anything else, because we need to know the answer to the question of how we can know God.

Tearing pages out of our diary

For that reason, this story helps us to think about our busyness. It doesn't tell us not to be busy. Rather, it asks us to think about whether we've missed something: the one thing we need – a relationship with God through Jesus. It pushes us to consider whether in being responsible people we've ignored God.

Let's think about being busy for a moment. We know that being good women means to be busy in our culture. It means, most likely, that we are fulfilling responsibilities. We're being good employers or employees; good daughters or wives or sisters or friends; good mothers or grandmothers or aunts; good citizens or householders. We're busy people often because we are being responsible people.

But even in our busyness, we'll let everything drop – we'll tear pages out of our diary – if someone we love needs us.

A few years ago just before Christmas, my husband's grandfather was taken to hospital, very ill. My husband dropped everything, and was able to be with him for that week before he died. It meant that all our Christmas plans were put on hold, and ultimately cancelled. But our plans for Christmas weren't as important as my husband being with his grandfather and family. So we tore pages out of our diary because of an important relationship.

We all do this. If a friend gets taken to hospital, we'll take time out to be with them and help them. If someone we love gets married, we'll take time out to celebrate with them and help in the preparations. We don't suddenly become irresponsible if we make choices like those. There are times when a person is more important than our busyness. And when we do rip pages out of our diaries, so to speak, for those important people and relationships, we often find that it gives us a perspective on our busyness. It helps us understand something of the bigger picture of our lives. It helps us realise that the important people in our lives are the reason for much of our busyness.

Because Jesus is here

What Jesus is saying to Martha here is that *he* is that person more than anyone else. He tells Martha that she needs to rip the day out of her diary because *he* is here and she needs to listen to him.

Why is Jesus *this* important? Because Jesus is the only way to God.

It is Jesus who died on the cross, because we have treated him badly and God is angry with us. It is Jesus who takes our place so that we can come to God. It is Jesus who shows us by dying and rising again for us how much God loves us. It is Jesus who takes this, our unsolvable problem, and solves it.

That's why Mary was listening to Jesus. Not just because she liked him or because she wanted to think about philosophical questions or something else. No, Mary was listening to Jesus because he, more than any other, can make sense of our busyness and put it all in perspective. Mary was listening to Jesus because neither she nor we can come to God by ourselves.

So, in this story, Martha wasn't being reprimanded because she was too busy. Jesus longed to tell her the good news – that God had sent him to bring her back to God. He wanted her to understand what he would do in dying and rising again for her. He wanted her to follow him, even if it meant that she had to tear pages out of her diary to do it.

Clarity in our busyness

What does Jesus say about us and our busyness? The same

thing he said to Martha. He doesn't want us to be irresponsible in our relationships, but he does ask us – have we done the one necessary, clear thing? Have we sorted out our relationship with God – the one thing that is needed?

It's not enough to be responsible – an excellent daughter, employer, aunt, mother, citizen… That isn't the one necessary thing. What is necessary is that we do something about our relationship with God.

Jesus came into the world to die and rise again so that you and I could have a renewed relationship with God. This is what God asks us today – in the midst of our busyness. Do we have this relationship with God? The one necessary thing? We need to ask Jesus to make us right with God. He is the only one who can.

Have you taken the time yet to find out more about Jesus? Have you read or heard what he said and did? Read the rest of Luke's story of Jesus and find out more. Don't let the chance to find out about Jesus pass you by because you have too much on.

If you are reading this book, you have already started to think about Jesus. Keep on reading and investigating. Talk about what you are reading with a Christian you can trust. Don't put this off because you are too busy. Be absolutely clear about what is important in life.

ENDNOTE
1. Luke 10:38-42

Love
Angela Cole

*M*y youngest boy is almost a year old – a remarkable age in a tiny life like his. In the blink of an eye, he's teetering on the edge of walking. A stop and start kind of thing, but almost ready to launch himself headlong into toddler-hood. Like a sponge, he's absorbing everything around him, parroting me as I teach him the usual party tricks so he can charm the big people around him with claps and waves and kisses. This once helpless little one who at first struggled to attach to my breast now relishes family food like a pro – grasping with both hands and screeching for more.

Yet as exciting as all this frenetic activity is for my son, there is nothing and no-one right now that compares with – *me*. I'm the centre of his busy world. He hears my voice from another room, and he'll drop everything, racing as fast as hands and knees can take him – just to see me. Around the corner, and he's found me, arms now reaching up with fingers opening and shutting frantically – lift me, Mummy, pick me up… So I reach down and swing him up into my arms. His body relaxes with a sigh and then he's sucking his thumb, eyes fixed on mine, content and secure.

See-sawing emotions

It tugs at my heart, this feeling of being loved so much. Sometimes, the huge space I fill in this little life overwhelms me, and I can't quite catch my breath – fearful and constricted by the responsibility of it all. But then I remember how quickly time is racing by, and I grieve for how short-lived this intense motherlove of his will be. All too soon, my baby will disentangle from me and become himself. He will grow strong and independent, and I will become ever smaller in his mind's eye.

See-sawing emotions, bittersweet experiences and contradictions – these are the things of motherhood… My passion for my children contrasts with my frustration when I'm wearied by the drudgery of meeting their needs round-the-clock. My pain at their birth fades into insignificance when I hold them in my arms – face to face at last after an eternity of waiting. My sense of utter helplessness when my babies won't stop crying belies the confidence and maturity I would ordinarily display! My home – cluttered and chaotic – gives the lie to the sense of order I prided myself on before kids! And I research and deliberate and discuss every aspect of child-raising – holding my breath, wanting to "do it just right" – only to find most of the time I'm "just doing it" – winging it, using my survival instincts and hoping for the best.

Smothered at times by their need of me, yet filled to bursting with love and that fierce maternal desire to protect them… How do I make sense of the jumble of feelings my kids evoke in me? For certain, becoming a Mum has made for big emotions – deep, strong ones that I can't easily control. My children colour every aspect of my life. One writer puts it this way: *"Motherhood consumes us, particularly in the early stages. Not just our energy, our routines and our time, but our focus as well. Our thoughts are ambushed…"*[1]

Giving good gifts

This powerful grip a woman's child clamps around her heart and mind is a marketer's dream. Skim through the advertising pages of any Mother and Child magazine with me:

- "They grow up so fast… *Absolute Photography*: Beautiful Natural Art"
- "Children should be seated first class! *Furniture that Grows…*"
- "There's only one term left to give your pre-school child a head start in life… Act Now! Enrol at *Ready to Read*."
- "Ever lost your child? Help is here! Stay alert with '*ChildGuard*' wireless child tracker"
- "Smart Kids Play Music… Give your child direction and the discipline to strive for a dream"

Who could resist? I *long* to give good gifts to my children! I *love* them and want only the very best for them – long life, perfect health, quality education, positive experiences… I will do anything to keep them safe, and am more than willing to make sacrifices so my children will thrive and fulfil their potential.

Yet although I'm an incredibly dedicated Mum, there are plenty of times when I let my kids down. Despite my best intentions, I'm nowhere near perfect. I lose my temper, break my promises and deal with them too harshly. I fumble for wisdom, make poor choices, focus on the wrong issues…

Even the most passionate motherlove can never overcome my failings. Just like me, my children will not be able to reflect honestly on their upbringing without dredging up some hurtful memories. And however desperately I try to fill up my kids' lives – with things, events, experiences – I'm fooling myself if I think these will truly satisfy them.

The perfect parent

Imagine, then, someone loving my children even *better* than I can! What if there were someone who could provide *perfectly* for them – someone who could anticipate and meet their deepest needs, not merely *longing* to give them the things that really matter, but actually able to *deliver* on the promise?

Jesus said that *God* loves His children like that.

> *"Which of you, if your son asks for bread, will give him a stone instead? Or if he asks for a fish will give him a snake? If you, then, though you are evil, know how to give good gifts to your children, how much more will your Father in heaven give good gifts to those who ask him!"*[2]

Jesus is speaking, here, to people just like me. Think about it, he reasons, you all-too-human parents who struggle with inconsistencies and selfishness. Even *you* would never dream of giving something unsatisfying or harmful to the child you love and who depends on you if he asks for something to satisfy a real need. So you can be *certain* that God, the Heavenly Father – who is perfect in every way and loves like no-one else can – will give good things to His children.

In their context, these words form part of a section where Jesus is teaching his disciples about prayer. Be encouraged, he says, because prayer to a loving Father is effective. God cares about those things that matter to His children, and His response – flowing freely out of His Fatherlove for them – is to bless them generously.

Clearly, here is an intimate relationship at work – a dependent child calling on the one who knows him personally, loves him dearly and intends what is best for him. As a Mum, I totally identify with this. I'm *living* it with my children every day!

But is it possible to have this depth of relationship with *God*? Who on earth can climb onto the Creator's lap and snuggle in close?

The Bible tells us that those who have faith in Jesus become precious members of God's family:

To all who received him, to those who believed in his name, he gave the right to become children of God.[3]

Do you see what the writer, John, is saying? God offers us the opportunity of a lifetime – to be transformed from mere acquaintances into daughters and sons, with all the status and privileges that would imply in a human family and so much more! Those who trust in Jesus can be *born anew* into the heavenly family.

We believe by receiving! We express our trust in God and our reliance on His promise simply by accepting His free gift – just as my children do when they reach out and take from me the lovingly-wrapped birthday present I have carefully chosen for them and waited with such excitement to watch them open!

To be God's child is to be *truly* loved – no holds barred and no let-downs.

The needs of God's children are always supplied out of the Father's wisdom.

God's children are eternally secure.

If you're anything like me, you long for those closest to you to experience fullness of life like this! Which of you wouldn't want this for yourselves?

My devotion to my own children – my motherlove – is actually just a shadow of God's passionate Fatherlove. Wrap yourself and your family up in it, safe and warm in loving arms!

How great is the love the Father has lavished on us, that we should be called children of God![4]

ENDNOTES
1. Kylie Ladd, 'Unfinished Symphony', *Sydney's Child*, October 2004
2. Matthew 7: 9-11
3. John 1: 12
4. 1 John 3: 1

Security
Christine Jensen

*H*ow did the horrific Asian tsunami affect you?

Did you feel sadness, despair, hopelessness, rage? The loss of so many lives was overwhelming. At first, it didn't seem to register, but as the newspapers and television made the events roll into our living rooms night after night we felt intimately involved. At times it was as though tragedy had arrived on our doorstep. This was certainly a Christmas we'd rather forget.

How do such events make you feel? The world is probably not as safe or secure as we once believed. Events like these make us wonder what is happening in the world. We see things happening we never imagined would happen. I'll never forget watching the television on September 11 2001 and seeing the planes crash into the World Trade Centre in New York. It was unbelievable. I thought I must have been imagining what I was seeing; perhaps it was a trailer for a forthcoming movie?

Our more personal worlds aren't always what we imagined they'd be either. We experience our own catastrophes. They arrive in the form of sickness, accident, financial worries or deep relationship problems. Insecurity can arrive suddenly at the door.

Several years ago, we were overjoyed at the news that our daughter was pregnant with our first grandchild. But as the pregnancy developed, it was obvious that something was wrong. The doctors told her that she would carry the baby to full term, but it would not live. When I heard that news, it seemed like a big black hole had opened up for me. I felt completely helpless. There was nothing I could do to make it better – which is what mothers are supposed to do.

Sometimes, however, our problems are more long term. We find that we're failing to balance the priorities of a husband, children, work and managing the home in all its complexities. Or we find relationships aren't quite what we expected. Likewise, as children grow into adolescents, they bring new and often frightening challenges.

Even if we have lived without any consideration of God, our personal worries, anxieties, struggles, tensions, fractured relationships, failing health and difficulties often force us to reconsider what life is all about. We may ask the question afresh, "Is there a God? Where is he? How could God let this happen to me? Does God have anything to say to us in this frightening world?"

Although you may find it hard to believe, God *is* actually there. And he hasn't left this world to its own devices, spinning out of control. He is intimately involved in its care and control. More than that, he lets us know what he is like and what he is doing. How?

One answer is that he has revealed himself through the creation of the world. Simply by looking around us we can tell that God exists, and that he is powerful and worthy of our worship. In creation we see the incredible majesty and power of God. But it is hard for us to know much more about him than that.

We need God to speak to us, and he has done so. He has made himself known through his Son, Jesus, who perfectly shows us what God is like. The Bible is the written record of

God at work through his people and his Son. When we read it, we see how relevant it is to life in this insecure world.

Let's explore three major aspects of what God is like.

God is in charge

The Bible says, 'The Lord is the everlasting God, the creator of the ends of the earth. He will not grow tired or weary.'[1] Think what this means: he created…well, *everything* – all that we see or experience which is part of his creation. And more than that: he keeps it all going.

Sometimes this troubles us. Why has he allowed some painful thing to happen, we ask, if he is in charge? Sometimes it is because of the evil perpetrated by men and women – such as September 11. Often we do not know why, since he has not told us. But we live in a world that has declared God *persona non grata*, and the result is that things inevitably go wrong. Yet surely it is better to believe that he is in charge and has a reason for what has happened, rather than there being no one in charge, and it is all an accident.

We can never hide from God – although we often like to think that we can do just that. The Bible gives us an amazing picture of who God is. None can compare to him! The Bible calls him "everlasting": he lasts from before time to after the end of time.[2] When I think how tired I feel sometimes after a long day, to know that God is never weary helps me to press on.

He is in control. He hasn't just left the world spinning without direction and purpose. In another part of the Bible, we read 'He works everything out in conformity with the purpose of his will.'[3] This tells us that life has a meaning and that God is powerful enough to bring his plans to pass.

When I suffered a number of miscarriages and was extremely sad about the loss of our little ones, I knew I was not on my own. I turned to him. I have no idea why these losses happened. But I found that I knew enough about God to trust him with the 'why' question.

The Bible taught me that he knew my every need. He cared for me and wanted only the best for me. Even at the very beginning of our human life, before we were born, he knew us.[4] He certainly knew the babies that I had never known. I may not have known 'why', but I knew his peace.

What are the implications of God being in charge? It is the foundation of how we think about everything. Life now has a direction and purpose. It affects how we think about the events that are happening in the world, the decisions we make, matters of life and death, how we bring up our children and even how we spend our money. If God is God, the Creator who is in charge, we can live with hope in a fractured world.

But what about the tsunami, the violence in the world, or the pains and sadness we experience in our own lives? Unfortunately, because we live in a world that has turned its back on God, events like this overtake us from time to time. God doesn't say they won't happen, but that he will keep us and sustain us in the midst of them. He is the everlasting God, far greater than we can ever imagine. Furthermore, he has promised that in heaven, he will wipe away every tear.[5]

God is faithful

That means he is dependable and reliable. Rock-like. He is true to his Word. The Bible tells us that he is completely faithful. This means that – unlike anyone else we know – he will never let us down. We are able to trust him utterly. Living with someone who tells untruths all the time is very difficult. You learn not to trust the person, and it is hard to keep loving them.

God is completely different. It's hard to think what that could be like, but he is unreservedly consistent. How we are doesn't change him. The Bible tells us that God does not change like shifting shadows. When the world proves deceptive and untrue, God remains true.

What does this mean? When we are uncertain and doubt and are not sure what's happening or what life is all about, God is true to his word. We all have doubts from time to time. We all have questions about God and what he is doing. But, we should not let doubts overwhelm us. Why not try talking to him about those doubts? He longs for us to come to him like that.

God is forgiving

The Bible describes him as a *'forgiving God, gracious and compassionate, slow to anger and abounding in love.'*[6] What great news this is! No matter who you are, no matter how respectable your life has been, there are things in it to regret. Our own conscience tells us that. So does the word of God. If we compare ourselves with what God tells us about how we should live, the result is a failure for us. Every single person needs forgiveness from God.

Sometime we may even think that our sins are too great for God to forgive. I remember meeting a person who was tormented because he had done something earlier in his life which gave his conscience no rest. But the truth is nothing we ever do or think can keep us from coming to God, because he longs for humans to have a relationship with him. He has promised that anyone who owns up to his sin and rebellion (this is called confessing) will be forgiven by him.

God has provided forgiveness through his Son, Jesus. When Jesus was put to death, he was suffering our punishment. He was acting on our behalf, so that we would not need to be condemned for our faults. Confessing our sins means telling God that we've been living our life without even considering him, that we've been self-centred and that we haven't been trying to please him at all.

There are some people who have experienced such great hurts that they feel unable to forgive those who have offended them. We know that in some families there are people who haven't spoken to each other for years. How can they possibly forgive? In some ways, forgiveness is a process, which may take a long time to be worked out. Knowing that we have been forgiven by God ourselves can give us the courage to begin this process, even though reconciliation may never be possible.

Forgiveness is a remarkable gift. It gives us the capacity to change. It enables us to start again, to put the past behind us, to carry no more grudges and to experience God's mercy. There's nothing we can do to earn God's forgiveness. We merely have to ask. That sometimes means acknowledging that without God, we can do nothing to please him. It means committing ourselves to him.

When we're surrounded by a world uncertain of its direction and purpose, we too might find ourselves wondering what life is all about. Knowing that God's in charge, is faithful and is forgiving does give a framework for thinking about what is crucial for a secure life.

There will be times when the pains, disappointments and frustrations seem almost too much to bear, but God himself never goes away. We have a God who stands with us in all of life's circumstances, and says "Come to me". We are not on our own. He has sent his own Son, Jesus, for us. He doesn't give up on us, grow tired or weary, but knows our every need, our worries, our stress points and our anxieties. Trusting Jesus is the security we're searching for. He knows our inmost thoughts and deepest longings. Whatever happens, he remains constant.

You might be challenged after reading this to ask yourself: what part does God have to play in my life as I face the complexities of the world and my own mortality? These are big questions which we all need to ask. The way forward is to make sure that you are listening to him as he speaks to you in his Word, especially what he has to say about Jesus – and trust what he tells you.

ENDNOTES
1. Revelation 4:1
2. Isaiah 40:25,28
3. Ephesians 1:11
4. Psalm 139:13
5. Revelation 21:4
6. Nehemiah 9:17

Isobel's **story**

My story about becoming a Christian really begins with my mum.

Born in Malaysia, she grew up in a very superstitious family. Her mother miscarried a number of times before having my mum; this was seen as the gods stealing the babies away. As a result, Mum grew up calling her parents 'Aunty' and 'Uncle' so that the gods would be fooled and not realise that she was actually their daughter. That sort of superstition was found in every sphere of her life. In Chinese religion, there is a god known as the 'God in heaven.' When she got into trouble, Mum would kneel at her bedroom window, looking out to the sky, and pray to this 'God in heaven' asking him to help her. The members of her family are still superstitious in the extreme; one of her relatives is even a medium to the dead.

My mother was educated in a Roman Catholic school in Malaysia, although she does not remember learning much about Jesus at all. She can remember asking what Jesus did to deserve to die; her impression was that he must have been a very bad man to deserve to die in such an awful way.

When she was about 19 she left home and went to train as a nurse in Singapore. As it happened, her room-mate was a Christian and took her to an old-fashioned revival meeting. The preacher preached a 'hellfire and brimstone' kind of sermon and my mother became a Christian. Her superstitious background had made her a bit of a scaredy-cat, so the news that Jesus would rescue her from God's judgment was tremendously welcome. Even now she can remember the wonderful sense of relief that she didn't need to be afraid of the dark anymore.

Her Christianity grew from that sudden conversion. Although at the time it was certainly the last thing that she or any members of the family expected, we can see now that God answered those first prayers that she prayed as a child. The unknown 'God in heaven' made himself known to her though Jesus.

In the 1960's, she emigrated and married my dad, who was also a Christian. Consequently, I grew up in a Christian home. As neither of my parents had grown up in a Christian home, they felt very much in the dark when it came to raising us as believers. They were very keen, but felt like they didn't really know how to go about it. Mum tells me that their main strategy was to pray. She said they prayed continually that God would work within us and that we would grow up with our faith in Christ.

As I look back on our home, Christian life and practice were part and parcel of my learning and growth. I cannot remember a time when I did not participate in going to church and youth group and the other things that you do when you're growing up as a Christian. I would have been 25 before I first missed church on a Sunday morning. I can't think of a time when I did not know God and that God loved me or that I didn't know that Jesus had died for me. I didn't necessarily know what that meant, but I grew up in it. I don't think I was born a Christian but I can't pinpoint an exact time. You believe as a child, but as you grow your faith has to grow too.

At a number of different points I made a commitment to Christ as I was growing up. The most significant moment for me would have been at a Billy Graham meeting. I was about 14. Both my sister and I 'went forward'. This was one of the times when I was challenged to stand for Christ. That one sticks in my memory because it struck home that I needed to make my own choice about following Jesus. I couldn't just absorb it from my parents.

In high school, a lot of my friends left fellowship and church. As a result, I was less keen. I didn't turn away, but I felt lonely with my friends pulling out. I had never explored any doubts, but now little things started to come into my mind. 'Did my friends leave church because they found out that God didn't exist? Did they find out that it wasn't worth it?' I didn't talk about these thoughts with anyone, but they were there in the back of my mind.

These doubts and questions became more intense once I started university. A whole set of different friends and life experiences became available to me. Mum was very worried about me at this time! I started thinking very seriously about whether or not I really wanted to be a Christian. I recognized that if Christianity was true then I needed to give my whole life to following God, but if it was not true then it was not worth anything at all. There wasn't really any point in being half-hearted.

Before I could commit to being a Christian, there were a few things that I wanted to know. The reliability of the Bible as God's Word was one thing. I went to hear some lectures on the historical evidences for the Bible. Now that I was older I wanted to see some more substantive proof. The lecturer was very good. Speaking as an intelligent adult to intelligent adults, he provided evidence that gave me confidence that it was not silly to believe the Bible. Around this time, too, I read a book about the major world religions. It wasn't that I wanted to explore other religions thoroughly, but I wanted to know how Christianity was different from other faiths.

I also went to some lectures by philosophers who talked about Christian philosophy and the reasonableness of Christian ethics and belief. It was fantastic to hear people talking about Christian ethics. It helped me to grow up in my

Christian understanding. Knowing Jesus is Lord had deeper and more far-reaching implications than just the Sunday School stories about Jesus. I began to see how Christian faith changes everything we think and do. Christianity is much more grown-up and reasonable than I thought. It's not just children who believe in God.

The first two years of university were the critical time for me. If there was a crucial turning-point, it would have been the time that I read the book of Hebrews in the Bible. A friend challenged me to read it by saying that God's Word was the best thing to help me work out if I should be a Christian. Reading the book of Hebrews was just fantastic, especially the way that it made sense of the link between the Old Testament and the New Testament. There is a lot of encouragement there not to give up. You've run the race this far – keep going. At that point I was convinced. I knew that I wanted to keep following Christ.

Since then, life keeps bringing new challenges to my faith. Right after I got engaged I was sick with glandular fever and couldn't do anything. I had worked for a church for a number of years, and had studied for a year at Bible college. After being so active, I was now so tired I could hardly do anything, even pray. After I got a bit better I felt spiritually far from God. I felt like I was unfaithful. But this experience made me realise that my relationship with God was all about what God had done for me, not about what I could or couldn't do. You can't earn your way to heaven – you can't earn God's love. In the end, God loves us because he loves us, not because of what we can do for him. That was really important for me to learn.

Now, I am the mother of three little girls. The longer I am a parent, the more clearly I can see the mistakes that I make; in addition, so many things to do with our children are out of our control. Just like my mother did for me, I pray for them a lot. I keep praying that they will know Jesus and that God will make himself known to them.

Control
Jenny Salt

T here is a photograph sitting on the desk in my office which always brings a smile to my face. It is a picture of a group of residential women students taken a few years ago while they were studying at the college where I am on faculty. The photo was the request of some of the male students who asked the girls to gather on the grass in front of one of the lecture halls.

As a faculty member, what I didn't know was that this situation was the culmination of a series of practical jokes that had been building between the men and the women for weeks. Revenge was the name of the game, and somehow I had been caught up in it. We were all gathered, the photo was taken and then without warning we were surrounded at every turn…men everywhere, each with a bucket, a hose or some other method of dispersing water. And there was no escape! They even had other students on 'door duty' preventing any way of escape inside the buildings.

Now I enjoy watching water fights but I don't relish getting caught in the middle of one. And here I was in the thick of it. Soon, my worst fear was realised – a male student coming towards me with a hose. There seemed to be no escape. I had to think quickly. I looked at him and said… "NO!"

Could I count on my position of authority at the college to ensure obedience to my command? I must admit I wasn't sure if I could pull it off. But sure enough, with my confident "NO", the student looked at me, backed off and put the hose on one of the female students. By responding to my "NO", the student recognized my authority and the position I held within the college.

I was surprised that my authority held sway – and even more relieved! But the Bible tells us about a man who never doubted his authority, which was far greater. Indeed he was able to stop something much more threatening than a group of fun-loving students with a water hose. He demonstrated his authority and control over raging torrents of water. The man was Jesus – a man who has control over what matters.

Authority over a storm

In the Bible, we read about Jesus' authority calming a storm.

> *Then he got into the boat and his disciples followed him. Without warning, a furious storm came up on the lake, so that the waves swept over the boat. But Jesus was sleeping. The disciples went and woke him, saying, "Lord, save us! We're going to drown!"*
>
> *He replied, "You of little faith, why are you so afraid?" Then he got up and rebuked the winds and the waves, and it was completely calm.*
>
> *The men were amazed and asked, "What kind of man is this? Even the winds and the waves obey him!"*[1]

In the middle of this terrifying storm, Jesus demonstrated his authority and power over nature by literally telling it to stop – and it did! This authority and power caused his disciples to sit up and ask a very appropriate question: *"Who is this man?"*

Matthew's biography provides us with an eye-witness account of Jesus' life. Throughout his account, Matthew records what Jesus did and taught, his miracles, his death on the cross and his resurrection from the dead. When we gather all this information together, we assemble an amazing picture of the person of Jesus Christ.

This account of Jesus calming the storm contributes a significant amount of detail to that astonishing picture.

Let's go back briefly and join the disciples during the storm. Leading up to this storm, Jesus had been teaching the crowds by Lake Galilee about what it really means to live the way God wants people to live. Many people were attracted to Jesus, not only because of what he taught but because he taught with authority. His teaching, as well as the way he healed people with a word and a touch, attracted large groups of people wherever he went.

Now, as he looks around at the great throng that has gathered, Jesus tells his disciples to get the boat ready to cross to the other side of the lake. (This was probably to give Jesus an opportunity to teach the disciples quietly away from the crowd.) So that's what they do. He and his disciples get into a boat and start to head to the other side of the lake.

Matthew writes that a furious storm comes up. Large waves crash over their boat as they battle the wind and the pounding rain. It would have been a terrifying situation. The power of nature can be frightening and devastating. Anyone caught up in the fury of a storm will know just how powerless they are.

Real storms and movie storms

In 2003 and 2004, I spent a year studying at a college situated in the northern suburbs of Chicago in Illinois. In this particular area of the United States, the seasons are very distinct. Winter is very cold, summer is very hot, and spring and autumn also have a characteristic feel.

In spring, as the weather heated up, I experienced some amazing electrical storms – both beautiful and terrifying. I also happened to be living on the edge of the tornado belt! For a few weeks in May, there were many news reports of tornados ripping through areas of the state and there was one occasion when a tornado came very close to where I was living. The siren was sounded, signalling that a tornado was close and that it was time to get into a basement until it passed! Well, it actually never hit us, but it was quite frightening at the time.

At no time did anyone think to go outside and tell the storm to stop! It would have been ridiculous. The wisest thing was to find a safe place and wait out the storm.

However, the disciples caught in the storm on Lake Galilee don't have the option of going for cover. So what do they do? They cry out to Jesus to do *something*. It is not clear what they want Jesus to do! However, Jesus does something that completely surprises them. He stands up and commands the wind and the waves to be still. In other words, he says, 'NO'. And it is completely calm. It's as if the switch for the storm is turned off.

It reminds me of the movie, *The Truman Show*. Truman, the main character of the movie, is born and adopted by a TV corporation, and this corporation creates a virtual life for Truman. Truman's whole world is a massive movie studio. Truman isn't aware, but there are hidden cameras everywhere, and the rest of the world turns on the television to watch Truman's life. And all the people in his life – his parents, his friends and even his wife – are actors playing a part.

The person in control of Truman's life is Christof, the head of the corporation. Christof controls everything, even down to the weather. In one of the last scenes in the movie, Truman is in a boat on the "lake" trying to escape this make-believe world and Christof sends a storm to stop him. Just as easily, Christof then turns the storm off. Christof is literally playing God, with his power to turn nature on and off.

Of course, *The Truman Show* is only a movie and Christof a character in the movie. In the real world, it is God who has the power to do this. No-one else can control nature. All our sophisticated technology may help to warn us, but we are simply unable to control it.

Jesus' authority

And that is exactly what the Bible says. There are parts of the Bible that describe God calming the powers of nature with a word. And on Lake Galilee, we saw Jesus doing just that. Jesus said "NO" to the storm and it immediately obeyed.

And so in this account, we are given a crucial piece of the puzzle of Jesus and his identity... *Jesus is Lord over creation. He is in control.*

So, what's the point of this particular eye witness account? Just who is Jesus and how does he affect how I live *my* life in the 21st Century? Are we in control of everything in our lives? I think as women in particular, being in control of our individual worlds is very important. Unfortunately, with busy lives and complicated relationships, we can feel like we are increasingly out of control. So there is great relief in knowing the one who *is* in control and has demonstrated his authority over this world – not just over nature, but life and death as well.

Acknowledging Jesus' control

So how do we respond to the One who is able to calm storms with a word?

We might be a bit like the disciples who asked, *"What kind of man is this? Even the winds and the waves obey him!"* At this stage, they didn't have a complete understanding of who Jesus was. But as they spent more time with Jesus, asking questions and thinking about everything that Jesus said and did, they began to understand more clearly.

A little later, Jesus asked them who they thought he was. Peter answered, *"You are the Christ, the son of the living God."*[2]

Peter was making a big statement here. Finally he recognised who this man was. Jesus – his friend and leader for nearly three years – was not just any man, but 'the Christ'.

'The Christ' was a term loaded with anticipation, describing God's promised ruler of his world, somebody with all of the authority of God himself. And Peter understood – this was exactly who Jesus must be. Who else could have authority over nature like this?

What about us?

If Jesus is the one with all God's authority – and indeed the author of life – yet we deny him any role in our life by ignoring him, we have a problem. We close ourselves off from access to all the good things he offers us as well. There are consequences for living in this way. Ultimately, the Bible tells us, we will be separated from him forever. But the Bible also tells us that Jesus took that penalty upon himself when he died on the cross. And God showed his acceptance of Jesus' sacrifice in our place, by raising him to life again, where he now rules over the entire world with all authority.

The Bible also says that God so loved the world that he gave his only son so that anyone who believes in him would not perish but have eternal life[3]. Just as Jesus had the authority to calm storms and heal diseases, he has the power to *bring life*, and life in abundance.

Jesus is Lord and the only proper response is to believe in him.

But these things are written so that you may believe that Jesus is the Christ, the Son of God, and that by believing you may have life in his name.[4]

ENDNOTES
1. Matthew 8:23-27
2. Matthew 16:16
3. John 3:16
4. John 20:31

Acceptance
Lesley Ramsay

I stood in front of my wardrobe, doors flung open. As my eyes flitted along the rack full of clothes, the question formed in my mind. It is the question that has risen in the mind of every woman – what will I wear? I was going to the wedding of a good friend's daughter where there would be a lot of not-seen-for-a-long-time friends. But the question seemed ridiculous. There were plenty of clothes staring back at me. Of course I had perfectly good clothes to wear. What was going on in my mind?

It is an evident truism – for good or bad – that we live in a world where appearance counts. Clothing has little to do with function, and more to do with adorning our bodies and making an impression on those we meet. The fashion industry is built solidly on this premise.

Fashion, plastic surgery and stilettos

Do you remember Jennifer Lopez in the recent chick-flick *Maid in Manhattan*? She's a kind and hard-working chambermaid in a ritzy Manhattan hotel, where she is ignored and snubbed by the wealthy patrons. One day, she tries on a Dolce and Gabbana suit that belongs to a guest, and meets the handsome, wealthy hunk played by Ralph Fiennes. He, who would not have given her a second glance before, is now captivated. All because of a posh frock!

Not only are we fixated with what we put on our bodies, but also with what our bodies look like.

Early in 2004, China hosted the Miss Ugly Contest. The contestants were fifty unattractive women. The top prize? $16,500 worth of plastic surgery. A 26-year-old translator, Zhang Di, won on the basis that her appearance would most benefit from plastic surgery. She was reported as saying that her appearance stopped her from getting ahead in life.

She is not the only one. There are millions of people all over the world who cannot stand their own faces or even their whole bodies. Plastic surgery is now a booming industry around the world. Husbands give their wives facelifts as birthday presents, competitions offer nose jobs as prizes. Women allow total strangers to drill and slice, scorch and burn away old skin, suck stuff out, inject other stuff, cut and pull and stitch, extract teeth – all in the name of impressing others. There's even a surgical podiatrist in America who shortens women's toes so they will look good in open-toed stilettos.

Now you probably don't go to these lengths, but we all understand the reasoning behind the thinking. We all care about our appearance because we long for acceptance. We long to have others look at us and befriend us, to know us and to love us.

But what would happen if our appearance was freakishly affected by an accident or disease? Listen to these women who have all suffered some form of facial disfigurement:

"I am sure that if I felt happier with people I could get them to see beyond the way I look and get to know the real me."

"I am okay with people that I know really well, but I just clam up as soon as there is anyone there that I haven't met before."

"I am all right until someone mentions my face, and then I feel really embarrassed and just want to go home."

"I'm always on edge in social situations in case someone asks what happened to me."

Of course they will all have friends and family who will look beyond the grotesque, and love them for who they are. But the reticence and fear remain. We ache for a basis of acceptance that has to do with who we are, rather than what we look like.

God's beauty contest

If God had a beauty contest, what would it be like? Is God interested in what I look like or what I wear? Does he care if my face is disfigured or not? How does God see me? How do I measure up in his eyes? Is he suitably impressed with my appearance?

There are answers to those questions. In the Bible, God says:

Do not consider a person's appearance or his height... The LORD does not look at the things man looks at. Man looks at the outward appearance, but the LORD looks at the heart.[1]

A few years ago, I was invited to a friend's engagement party. It was her second marriage and I hadn't seen her for a while. When I arrived, I hugged her and then asked where her fiancée was. She pointed out a group of men on the other side of the room, and with a grin on her face, asked if I could guess which one he was. I perused the group – there was a tall and handsome one, a very intelligent one with rimless glasses, a not so handsome but very homely one, along with a couple of, well, nondescript men. I must have looked perplexed, because with a glint in her eye, she said "It's him" and pointed to one of the nondescripts – a short balding man. He certainly didn't look like the man my friend would marry. How wrong I had been.

People often fall into the same trap. We judge, we accept or reject, on the basis of what we see. Ponder again those terrific words…

> *The LORD does not look at the things man looks at. Man looks at the outward appearance, but the LORD looks at the heart.*

Two reactions – relief and fear

I don't know about you, but when I read these words, I have two reactions.

The first is relief. Thank goodness for that! This is great news for someone who is very ordinary, who is beginning to display the effects of aging, who has floppy underarms and blotchy skin. I may scour the beauty pages for the latest techniques and products, and shop-till-I-drop so that I can try and impress other people with what I wear, but I don't have to impress God because God doesn't look at the outward appearance. He doesn't care what I look like. He just cares about my heart.

Besides, while I may not be able to impress God in the fashion stakes, I sure could impress him with the good things I do. I could recite off a whole list of things: I'm a good mother; I don't cheat on my husband; if I win the Lottery I'll happily give some to friends in need or the Red Cross; I help out at the kids' school with canteen or reading; I'm not a paedophile or a mass murderer. I admit I'm not perfect, but when God looks at my heart, surely he can see that I'm good enough.

My second reaction is more guarded – tinged with a little fear. What is it that God looks at? My *heart* – the real me, deep down inside where nobody else sees. That makes me worry. Yes, I may do good things, but I also know what I can be like deep down inside. It's not all shining light in my heart. There's a dark side to me, just as there's a dark side to you. There's a dark side to everyone.

We see it most starkly when 4 hate-filled terrorists kill over 50 people by blowing themselves up in London. Conversely, it is also clearly visible when the house of a peaceful Moslem family is daubed with graffiti that says, "Go home, we don't want you here." But we also see it in the playground of every school every day in taunts like, "We hate you, you can't play with us. You're a sissy, we're going to get you after school." These aren't terrorists, these are our children.

And what about us? We may not kill anyone or blurt out that we hate them, but sometimes in our *hearts* that's what we do. We often want people to hurt like we're hurting. At times we want revenge. Occasionally we get jealous when someone else gets something we think we deserve. We lie, we may look down on other people or cheat on our tax returns. And there are other things, too, which I can't name. But they are there in your heart. You know what they are. They are in my heart, and I'm too embarrassed to write them down. But I am absolutely sure that God sees them.

That's when I get worried. What if when God looks at my heart, the dark side of my heart overwhelms the good things I do? How do I know if the good is good enough? Do you know what people tend to do in this situation? We look around and compare ourselves to other people. If we look long enough, we can always find someone who is not as good as us. Mother Theresa? No. But my next door neighbour? Yes, I beat her hands down. Yet still the thought nags me – is my 'good' good enough? It's a very big risk I am taking. I need to know: what is God's standard?

Reaching the qualifying standard

In the year before each Olympic Games, every athlete knows they have to reach a specific qualifying standard before they can be considered for selection. It may be running a certain time in the last 12 months, or reaching a particular height in the National Championships.

Early in 2004, I read about Kyle Vander-Kuyp, an Australian hurdler. At the Nationals, he had posted a time of 13.65 seconds for the 110 metres hurdles. However the qualifying time for the Athens Games was 13.55 seconds. A mere tenth of a second, a blink of an eyelid! Surely this would be enough. But that cut no ice with the selectors.

It's no use an athlete saying, "Well, I think my time is good enough, I think I'll make it onto the team". He or she has to find out what the qualifying standard is, and reach it.

The same is true for us. We have to find out what God's standard is.

Fortunately the Bible answers that question for us. We can know the answer. The Bible tells us that God's standard is absolute perfection, one hundred per cent. It tells us that we are to love God with *all* our heart, *all* our soul, *all* our mind and *all* our strength. We are to honour him as God, adore him, obey him. Completely. The tiniest deviation from this standard, the smallest flaw, disqualifies you.

I know I don't do that. I don't reach the standard. *I* really want to be 'god' in my world.

This sub-standard attitude to God is reflected in sub-standard behaviour towards my fellow humans. Even if I was disciplined and good enough to restrict myself to only one wrong thought, one selfish action, one mean word per day (and I can assure you, I'm not), then by now I would have totalled up more than 56,000 mistakes. I'm well short of the qualifying mark. So, in actual fact, I can't stop worrying because I'm in big trouble. If this is the qualifying standard – where the bar is set – and I can't reach it, then my 'good' is not good enough. I can't impress God with my appearance and I can't impress him with my heart either. This falling short of God's standards is what the Bible calls sin or rebellion against God.

When I first made this discovery, I thought "this isn't fair – nobody is perfect, nobody can be good enough. Everybody is a rebel. Nobody gets the tick of approval from God. Not even someone like Mother Theresa was perfect. Do you mean SHE doesn't even meet God's standards?"

That's right; nobody meets the standard… except one man.

Jesus meets the standard

What I have said may seem like pretty depressing news. But the good news is, this one man makes all the difference. Because that man is Jesus, and he was perfect. He always and completely loved, honoured and obeyed his heavenly Father. He treated God as if he was God. So, he never cheated, never lied, never hated, never thought or did or said anything wrong.

And then one Friday afternoon, 2000 years ago, he was nailed to a cross and was crucified. The Bible tells us why that happened. Our failure to reach God's standard is highly offensive to God, and he declares that it must be judged and punished. But because of God's great love for us, he wants to rescue us from that judgement. Because Jesus was perfect, he was able to take the punishment that our sin and rebellion deserve, and to forgive us.

When I tell God that I'm really sorry for the appalling way that I've treated him, and that I want to be forgiven – that I want to throw my lot in with him – he welcomes me into his family and says that I am one of his. He does this by making my heart right. Jesus knew I couldn't make it on my own with God – my heart was too bad. So he gives me *his* goodness! Isn't that stunning? He could have just cut me loose and said, "If you're not going to meet my standards, then we may as well go our separate ways, and you'll end up separated from me forever."

But he didn't. He sent his son to die so that I could have his goodness to replace my bad heart, and become friends with him.

God's catwalk

Imagine that you are standing in front of God. The whole of humanity is there with you. And as each person passes before God, what does he see? He doesn't take any notice of their clothes, their weight, their body shape, their make up. Nor is he concerned with their job, or their status. He looks at their heart. And when I pass in front of him, because I've said that I'm sorry and asked him to forgive me, and trusted in the death of Jesus, he doesn't see my rebellion, my sin, all that imperfection and the dark side of my heart. What does he see? He sees Jesus' goodness, Jesus' perfection and says, "She is welcome!" It doesn't mean I'm perfect, but it does mean I am perfectly forgiven.

What does God see when he looks at your heart?

ENDNOTE
1. 1 Samuel 16:6-7

Debbie's story

The thing I remember most about my childhood was my mother's strong faith in God. We were a large but happy family – Mum and Dad, three brothers and one sister. Every night Mum would read the Bible to us and pray for, and with, each one of us.

I remember going to Sunday School and Girls' Club from a very young age, and knowing that God was very important. I didn't think about Him a lot – He was just part of life. He was just there! I knew that God loved me, but what I thought He wanted from me were acts of obedience, like being good and going to church. I certainly had no sense of Him being my friend.

When I was about 14, I started hanging out with a different crowd of kids. Now, going to church was no longer just a duty, but a real hassle. Bible reading at night was boring and an inconvenience. Being Christian was just too hard, and irrelevant. Going out with my friends was much more exciting. Much to my Mum's disappointment, I started moving away from God.

I was married at 18 and had a baby not long after. My husband couldn't handle such a responsibility and he began drinking heavily and became violent. As a consequence, my marriage lasted only 3 years.

During this tough time, I had drifted so far from God that He just didn't enter my thinking. My Mum would say "Debbie, why don't you pray about it?" But for me that would have been a sign of weakness. I was tough. I could handle this by myself. It got to the point that when Mum started talking about God, I would mentally turn off.

I moved back to a small flat at the back of my parents' house after the separation from my husband, and Mum kept asking me to come to church with her. I would go every now and then, just to keep her happy and off my back for a few weeks. I also started taking my daughter, Kylie, to Sunday School. Somehow, I knew it was important for her, but failed to see my own need of God.

In my mind, I always thought I would become a Christian when I was old and grey. I'd have my life now, enjoy myself, do what I wanted to do, and *then* I would commit myself to God. I definitely had the sense that I could do a better job of running my life than God could. It was certainly more fun my way. It was just too hard to be good all the time. It never occurred to me that what God offered me was a relationship.

Much later I remarried, and Mum and Dad bought a house next to my new husband and me. I was very happy and seemingly content with my lot. Mum continued going to church and Bible Study every week, occasionally dragging me along to dinners and special guest services at church. Mum also continued to be my best friend. We had lived close to each other virtually all my life. We would sit under the pergola at the back of my house and have a cup of coffee together almost every day.

But in June 1997, my life was turned upside down. The previous November, Mum had become sick. After countless tests and scans and misdiagnoses, we found ourselves sitting in the consulting rooms of a specialist. He told us that Mum had a tumour in her pancreas. It was inoperable and she probably had about 10 months to live. I remember being totally silent for several minutes – I think I was in shock. But then I exploded. I saw my comfortable world and my comfortable relationship with my mother being ripped apart. I was angry and I took my anger out on the doctor. I cried and yelled at the poor man. How could he have let this happen? They had wasted six months and something could have been done to save Mum. During my tirade, Mum had been sitting quietly, and at this point she put her arm around my shoulder and said, "It's all right, Debbie. Don't be sad for me. I'm going to see my Lord's face. I've been waiting for this all my life."

I couldn't understand how she could be so calm and accepting while I was a total mess. The following Sunday, her minister interviewed her in church. He asked her if she was afraid of anything. She replied in much the same way as she had in the doctor's rooms. No, she was not afraid of dying. After all, she was going to see Jesus and that would be terrific! The one thing she feared most was pain. She didn't know how she was going to cope with the pain. After the interview, a whole lot of people came out, put their hands on Mum and prayed for her. I remember that they prayed for her to be healed if that was what God wanted, and that she would be able to cope with any pain. Many of her friends were in tears at the end of the service, and I saw how much these people loved her too.

But as the reality began to set in, I got angry at God. I bombarded him with questions. How could you let this happen to my mother? She's been a Christian all her life, she's done everything you told her to do. How could you repay her like this? You can't take her from me. I need her. You have to cure her! I oscillated between being angry with him and begging him to heal Mum.

In the end, Mum didn't live 10 months. The time from diagnosis to death was only 10 weeks. In one sense, the time flew by; in another, it crawled by in slow motion. I took leave from work so I could take Mum to doctors' appointments and just be with her. During one period, she was hospitalised for about 10 days, and I stayed with her for the whole time. She would often say to me, "Read me the Bible, Debbie." She would tell me which parts to read, and she would lie back with her eyes closed and just listen. I would tell her to not accept dying, that God had to heal her. I remember her reply, "Yes Debbie, God is the only one who can heal me. But that may not be what he wants. If he doesn't, I accept that completely."

The next time she went to hospital turned out to be the last. She was quite weak now, and slept a lot. I spent hours and days just sitting by her bed. I watched as her friends from church visited and prayed for her. I remember her whispering to her minister one day, with a twinkle in her eye, "I'm going to see Jesus before you do!"

I had a lot of time to think. It was obvious that Mum was not afraid of dying. In actual fact, she seemed to be looking forward to it. I remember thinking how wonderful it would be not to be afraid. I knew she was going to heaven – there was no doubt in my mind about that. But then it hit me – I didn't have the same relationship with God that she does. What did this mean for me? I knew enough about the Christian faith to realise that unless I trusted in God, then heaven was out of the question.

Conversations I'd had with Mum came flooding back into my memory. I remember one where I had said that as long as I was a good person – friendly and helpful – then I would surely go to heaven. Mum had gently corrected me and stressed that it was the personal relationship with Jesus that was the important thing. As I looked at her, I realised she had that relationship, and I didn't.

That meant there was only one other place for me – hell. I became very frightened. I remember thinking, "I'm forty, and I have never thought about my mortality. What if I don't make it to old age to become a Christian? If I died tomorrow, I would go to hell!"

There was another thing that happened in those last days in the hospital. I'd been so angry with God because he was going to put her through all this pain; and she was afraid of the pain. But I actually saw with my own eyes that he protected her. The nurses would come into her room and offer her morphine because, in their words, "You must be in a lot of pain." But her face showed no sign of pain, in fact she was quite peaceful. She would tell the nurses: "I don't need it. I've got no pain – I've got God". It was astonishing. Here I was cursing God because he had given my mother this painful disease, yet he had answered her prayer and was faithfully protecting her.

All of this combined to make me very restless. My mind was buzzing with thoughts of death, with thoughts of never seeing Mum again, with thoughts of what a waste my forty years of life had been. I made up my mind I had to do something about it. It was now or never. This was Mum's last chance to get through to me that I needed to take the claims of Jesus seriously. It was time to stop running my own life. God knows I hadn't made a good job of it. I also had no control over when I would die. I had to do something and soon! But I didn't know what to do.

At Mum's funeral, I spoke to one of her friends. I knew she was a Christian and had been the leader of Mum's Bible study group. I told her I needed to talk with someone. She agreed to come and see me in two days time.

When she arrived, I just told her very simply that I wanted whatever it was that Mum had. I wanted something to look forward to – to no longer be afraid of death. I had ignored God for long enough, and I wanted to stop running and start living.

This woman, who later became my close friend,

explained that there were only two ways to live. One was to continue rebelling against the right of God to lovingly rule my life. The other was to submit to Jesus Christ as my Lord. The first would lead to judgement and separation from God after death; the second would lead to eternal life and a home in heaven with God.

The startling thing I learned was the significance of Jesus in all this. Of course, I had learned in Sunday School that Jesus had died on a cross and come back to life again. But I had never really understood the implications of what he had done. He hadn't died just because he was a martyr, but because he needed to pay the penalty for my rebellion (and everyone else's, too). He hadn't come back to life just to do another miracle, but to show that he had God's stamp of approval as the conqueror of death.

My friend put the question to me: which way do you want to live? The answer was as clear as crystal to me at that moment. For years I had fobbed off God (and my mother!), and was in real danger. That day, I knew there was no other decision I could make. I wanted to make a commitment to God. I wanted a personal relationship with him. I wanted his forgiveness.

I was aware just how vulnerable I was at this point in time. It had been less than a week since my mother had died, and I questioned myself as to whether I was just acting emotionally. Yet I knew what I was doing. There was a sense of urgency about getting this thing right. I needed to get right with God.

My friend suggested that I might like to think about it overnight. But I was desperate. I couldn't put this off a minute longer. And so together we knelt in the grass at the front of my place, and I asked God to forgive me for my forty years of rebellion, and thanked him for sending Jesus to die for me. I asked him to help me live for him.

I know that feelings are a poor indicator of the reality of

becoming a Christian, but at that moment, I felt as if a huge weight had been lifted from my shoulders. This was something I should have done years ago. God had been tugging and prodding, but I had just ignored him.

It was my disregard of God that really got to me. In the world's eyes I was not a bad person at all. In fact, most people would say I was a kind and caring person. But as far as I was concerned, I was the most rebellious person I knew. I had ignored God for forty years! How bad could you get? And to think that God loved me so much that He put His own son on the cross to die for people like me! It was mind-blowing.

Even now I still find that love hard to comprehend. There's a verse in the Bible which says, *"But God demonstrates his love for us in this: while we still sinners, Christ died for us."*[1] He continues to love people who are ignoring him and rebelling against him right now.

I have now been a Christian for five years. I am still growing and learning about Jesus, but the burden has gone. I have only one regret: that my mother could not share in the joy of my becoming a Christian. I remember a time when I went into her place and came upon her praying. She was saying, "Lord, please help Debbie to understand how much you love her, and how much she needs you."

In the end, God did answer her prayer. But it took her death to break through my stubborn will and make me realise my need of God.

I am eternally grateful to my mother for the example of her life, and the example of her death. One day I will see her in heaven and we will laugh together – and there'll be no more regrets.

ENDNOTE
1. Romans 5:8

Satisfaction
Sarie King

acquel Welsh, undoubtedly one of the greatest beauties of the twentieth century, once said, "Life is not what I expected. I've acquired everything I've ever wanted and yet I'm totally miserable!" She said, "I think that it is very peculiar that I can acquire wealth, fame and accomplishment in my career, have beautiful children and a lifestyle that seems terrific, and yet…be totally and miserably unhappy."

Now here's a woman that most women would love to be! By all appearances she seems to have everything – but none of it seems to satisfy.

What is it she expects of life that she feels she doesn't yet have?

Beautiful women, discontented lives

She's not alone. Marilyn Monroe, the blonde bombshell of the silver screen, stunned the world by declaring one day that she was incredibly lonely. Not long after that event she was found dead from an overdose, alone in her home.

Elizabeth Taylor – rich, beautiful and successful – told a TV interviewer recently how all her life she struggled with disappointment and alcoholism, and went through marriage after marriage in pursuit of that "one, happy, perfect and satisfying relationship".

What so disappointed these women about life and about relationships that they were destroying their lives and their bodies with drugs or alcohol to fill the void of their dissatisfaction?

And in case you're thinking that this 'dissatisfaction' is a generational thing, and that young celebrities have life easier…

You only need to pick up any women's magazine on the rack to read about J. Lo's continuing bitter feud with ex-fiancée Ben Afleck, how the young-married Brad Pitt and Jennifer Aniston have already split, why Uma Thurman divorced Ethan Hawke after only three years of marriage, and how Angelina Jolie has never recovered from her broken relationship with Billie Bob Thornton who left her with their newly adopted baby.

These magazines are an endless parade of dissatisfied lives.

But it's not only the rich and famous who struggle with the hope that life and relationships will bring them more.

I read recently that one woman endured a five-hour operation and suffered a painful post-operative ordeal in order to, as she put it, "iron the sags and wrinkles from my face".

Now this woman spent four years looking for the right doctor, paid more than £15,000 in expenses, stayed seven days in hospital, and said that during the days that followed the operation she felt as if "someone had blown her head up with a bicycle pump".

She had multiple stitches in her upper and lower eyelids, suffered a numbness in the ears, which may last up to six months – and still she was disappointed with the result!

Why would someone put themselves through that only to be disappointed in the end? Why? Because, as she put it, "I hope to be more attractive to men and so have better relationships!"

This woman was so dissatisfied with the way she looked, and so dissatisfied at her capacity to draw good relationships with the way she looked, yet she was still dissatisfied when she actually looked better!

In fact, she actually believed that you can expect better relationships the better you look!

Yet neither Racquel Welsh nor Elizabeth Taylor had better relationships. In fact, the more relationships they had, the more disastrous they were at them! Not to mention Uma, Angelina and Jennifer – some of the most beautiful women in the world.

Failed expectations

What is going on in our minds, our lives and in our relationships that we should be left so dissatisfied? Why are we so often left with failed expectations, yearning to look better, feel better, love better and be loved better?

Why is it that along with each of these people, we can end up saying life is not what I expected, this relationship is not what I expected, not having a relationship is not what I expected and disappointment is the last thing I expected?

Oscar Wilde once said, "There are only two tragedies in this world. One is not getting what you want, and the other is getting it!"

What he's implying is that when we do get what we want, we never seem to be happy with it. Our expectation is that we will one day be totally satisfied, but that day never seems to come. In fact, often the great expectation is a great disappointment.

What is the thing in your life that you would put at the end of a sentence which started: "If only…"? What would you say? What are you longing for, hoping for and striving for? Well, while you're thinking about that for a moment, let's turn to another story. It is a true story, this time from a biography of Jesus written by John, one of Jesus' close friends.

Disappointed with life

The story recorded here is about a woman not unlike us. Like so many of us, she is disappointed with life; it has not been all she'd expected and, during the motions of a fairly ordinary day, she comes across a man who would change her life forever.

Jesus was on his way to Galilee. He had to go through Samaria. So he came to a town in Samaria called Sychar. Jacob's well was there, and Jesus, tired as he was from the journey, sat down by the well.

When a Samaritan woman came to draw water, Jesus said to her, "Will you give me a drink?"

The Samaritan woman said to him, "You are a Jew and I am a Samaritan woman. How can you ask me for a drink?"

Jesus answered her, "If you knew the gift of God and who it is that asks you for a drink, you would have asked him and he would have given you living water."

"Sir", the woman said, "you have nothing to draw with and the well is deep. Where can you get this living water?"

Jesus answered, "Everyone who drinks this water will be thirsty again, but whoever drinks the water I give them will never thirst. Indeed, the water I give them will become in them a spring of water welling up to eternal life."

The woman said to him, "Sir, give me this water so that I won't get thirsty and have to keep coming here to draw water."

He told her, "Go, call your husband and come back."

"I have no husband", she replied.

Jesus said to her, "You are right when you say you have no husband. The fact is, you have had five husbands, and the man you now have is not your husband. What you have just said is quite true."[1]

An unexpected encounter

We find Jesus at this point on his way to a place called Galilee, and on the way we are told that he has to go through the town of Samaria. Now, geographically speaking, this is not actually true. In fact, there were several routes he could have taken to get to Galilee, but Jesus chooses to go through Samaria.

Why does he do this? Well, as the narrative unfolds, we discover that Jesus does this for one purpose and one purpose only, and that is to have a special encounter with this woman who lives in Samaria. From the beginning, we are told that this meeting is in fact no chance matter, but planned. You could say that it was 'destined' to happen.

Jesus goes through Samaria with the distinct expectation of meeting this woman, though of course, to her, the meeting seems quite by chance. It is totally 'unexpected'. Little does she know that God himself is bringing these two people together with the aim of fulfilling her quest.

A few years ago I watched a documentary on the stories of Holocaust survivors. Towards the end of the programme, they interviewed an elderly couple who had been married for over 45 years.

They were asked them how they met. The elderly man recounted the story of how, as a 16 year old Jewish boy, he was sent to a concentration camp in Poland. The camp was divided in two by a large barbed wire fence: women on one side and men on the other.

Comparatively, the men, on their side of the fence, were given hardly any food. He told how one young girl, seeing his emaciated state, took pity on him and would throw what little food she had over the fence each day, often going without herself.

Then one day the young boy came to their usual meeting place and told her that he was being transported to the death camps that very day and they would never see each other again.

Ten years later, after the war, having miraculously survived the death camps, and now a young man, he moved to America where a friend convinced him into a blind date. At first he did not recognise the beautiful Jewish woman who sat opposite him at the dinner table, but as they recounted their stories of the horrors of war, they discovered that they had been that young girl and young boy, and, in meeting again, that destiny had reunited them in extraordinary circumstances. And the rest is history…

We have all heard chance encounter or re-encounter stories, and we love to hear them because they say something which is inexplicable about life. And that is that amazing things happen – remarkable encounters with others that change the course of our life forever.

The meeting between this man Jesus and this woman at the well was no romantic one, but it was none the less deeply significant, and definitely no 'chance' matter.

This was no accident or twist of fate. This was meant to happen!

An unexpected offer

Why does Jesus come specifically to see this ordinary woman? It seems that he has something very unique which he wants to offer her! Jesus says to her:

> *"If you knew the gift of God and who it is that asks you for a drink, you would have asked him and he would have given you living water."*

In other words, if you really knew 'who' I was and exactly 'what' it is that I had to offer you, you would not be interested in these 'temporal' things such as drinking water, but you would ask for something which only I can give.

He says, in fact:

"Everyone who drinks this water will be thirsty again, but whoever drinks that water I give him will never thirst. Indeed, the water I give him will well up to eternal life."

Now this is probably the worst pick up line this woman ever heard, and she's no doubt heard a few in her time! But what is really happening here is a typical thing that happens in most relationships, where two people seem to be talking at 'crossed purposes' with each other. Jesus says one thing and the woman understands another.

Jesus is talking to the woman about 'spiritual thirst' and 'spiritual drinking', but the woman is so caught up in the 'literal' or 'physical' that she is not grasping what it is that he is really saying to her.

Jesus is making the single crucial point that whoever drinks of this 'physical water' will certainly thirst again, for that is the nature of the physical realm and that is the nature of humanity – nothing ever permanently quenches our thirst. You drink and you are satisfied, but then eventually you thirst again.

This is the nature of our world. The physical things in life were never created to be permanent, but temporary. They are only satisfying for a moment. Money, relationships, jobs, material possessions – no matter how much we have or how little we have, we do not find lasting satisfaction in any of those things. We will always want more. We will always search for something better and deeper.

Jesus says, *"Everyone who drinks from this water will thirst again"*. It is an absolute guarantee that we will go on to hunger and thirst again because that is the nature of those things.

In fact, in life we are to 'expect' the opposite! We are to 'expect' that these things will never totally satisfy us, for they are not built to satisfy what we truly need. It is our very 'dis-satisfaction' in life and relationships that is meant to indicate to us that we are searching for something far more significant and lasting. That satisfaction can only be met one way.

> *Jesus answered, "Everyone who drinks this water will be thirsty again, but whoever drinks the water I give him will never thirst."*

Jesus contrasts the 'physical thirsting' with what he has to offer. Jesus is telling the woman that it is futile pursuing satisfaction in earthly things that will never satisfy, when this thirst, this hunger you have in life, really only reflects a greater need that is not satisfied. That need is for 'spiritual relationship' and 'spiritual satisfaction'.

It is interesting to observe the way in recent years in which so many 'spring waters' and 'mineral waters' have flooded onto the market. People everywhere are buying 'water filters' and 'water purifiers'. Despite the fact that we have good water quality in the Western world, we are still obsessed with healthier and better water. It seems that once hooked on bottled water, water at home or from a tap will never satisfy in the same way ever again.

Jesus says that this is what he can give to men and women – not purified bottled water, but a water which tastes like nothing else and which quenches like nothing else, because it will quench a thirst so deep within that we will never again thirst for anything in the same way. We will be satisfied!

The woman says:

> *"Sir, give me this water so that I won't get thirsty and have to keep coming here to draw water."*

As you can see, the woman is still locked into the 'physical' and literal quenching of her thirst. So Jesus decides he will get to the 'heart' of the issue by revealing something about the nature of this woman and her 'real needs' which lack satisfaction. He says:

> *"Go, call your husband and come back."*
> *"I have no husband," she replied.*
> *Jesus said to her, "You are right when you say you have*
> *no husband. The fact is, you have had five husbands,*
> *and the man you now have is not your husband. What*
> *you have just said is quite true."*

Unexpected knowledge

By asking her this question, Jesus brings out into the open two critical things. First, having only just met this woman, Jesus reveals something about her private life that he could not possibly have known unless he was someone quite unique and was no 'ordinary man'. But he doesn't just reveal scintillating gossip about her private life. Rather he wants to reveal to her something he knows about her heart, something he knows about her need, her thirst.

Second, by laying bare her private life, it has exposed such dissatisfaction with life and relationships that she has been through five husbands already. Not only that, but that dissatisfaction of failed relationships has left her so empty that the man she is currently with, she has not even bothered to take as a husband. She's the Bible's version of Elizabeth Taylor.

Now, the failure of relationships to satisfy our expectations is not alien to our understanding, is it? I know that it has been my experience at times, and I doubt that anyone reading this hasn't known the pain and disappointment of hurt and broken relationships.

Several years ago, I saw a documentary on marriage

which said that 40% of first marriages fail, and 60% of second marriages fail. So considering this woman is now into her sixth relationship, the statistics for success are getting pretty low.

Of marriage, Andrew Lloyd Webber once said:

> *"We are hugely in love. We are driving everybody mad with our incredible love for each other."*

Just three short years later:

> *"It has become clear to me that, with great sadness, I have to now face that my marriage to Sarah Brightman is at an end."*

And Sean Penn, of his relationship with Madonna:

> *"I love her very much. … We desperately want to marry soon."*

Four years later, Madonna said:

> *"To hell with the cost, just get me a divorce and get it quickly."*

In Andrew Lloyd Webber, in Madonna and in the woman of Samaria, we see mirrored the common anguish of us all: failure to find total, lasting satisfaction in the things for which we had hoped.

But why is it that these relationships don't satisfy? Well, Jesus says that it is because we are all missing one crucial relationship in our lives. In fact, we are missing the one relationship which will truly satisfy, and that is 'relationship with him'.

In leaving God out of the picture in our lives, we put pressure on our partners to be something which they can never be: perfect. We put pressure on our partners to be like God to us – all loving, all caring, endlessly satisfying… But they can never be this and we should never expect that they can be like this. *We can't be like this!*

You see, no human relationship – no matter how wonderful, how promising – can ever be what God is meant to be for us, nor can any relationship ever substitute the relationship we were created to have with our creator.

In fact, human relationships can only ever be 'truly satisfying' when we 'let God be God and humans be humans'. When we expect our partners, parents, children or friends to be 'as God to us' then we are in trouble and so are our relationships.

Fulfilment of her greatest expectation

So, Jesus offers the woman a unique invitation. He says, "Come to me and ask for the water of life and you will not be disappointed. No. You didn't find satisfaction in those relationships, but 'come' and you will find satisfaction, lasting satisfaction, in me. Because what I have to offer you is perfect; it is permanent; it is eternal; it will satisfy. It will satisfy because it is the relationship after which you have truly quested. It is spiritual relationship. It is relationship with me."

But the woman struggles to grasp the full significance of what Jesus is now telling her. Maybe the conversation has become too personal or maybe she is confronted with the truth of her own empty existence. Whatever her reason, she suddenly pronounces with confidence that one day God's king, the Messiah, will come and when he does he'll be able to explain everything.

Then comes the stunning reply from the lips of Jesus: "*I am he. I am that Messiah. It is God himself who stands before you right at this moment. Come and find truth and fulfilment in me.*"

At that moment, she finally sees Jesus for who he really is. She abandons her empty water jar, races back to the town and declares to anyone who would listen, "*Come, I have found the one we have waited for: the Messiah.*" This unfulfilled woman had finally found the living water and her thirst is satisfied.

This woman, in this unexpected encounter, had received an unexpected offer which had truly fulfilled her greatest hope and longing. She had finally met the only one who could truly 'quench her thirst', who could 'truly satisfy'. And her relationship with God, and also with others, would be transformed forever.

Jesus' unexpected offer to this woman is the same offer he makes us today. For a world which hungers and thirsts for whatever will satisfy its deepest longings, Jesus is still the answer. He says to each of us, "**I am** the great life satisfier! I am able to give you life-giving water. **Come and drink from me.**"

ENDNOTE
1. John 4:4-18

Certainty

Ruth Muffett

*D*ana scanned the playground – where had Tom gone? She hadn't seen him for several minutes and was beginning to grow anxious. He had this incredible ability to disappear from under her nose – only to reappear half-a-heart-pounding-hour later. An enclosed slide finally spat him out. Dana relaxed and returned to our conversation.

"You know, I'm a good person, I haven't done anything too bad. What kind of a God would send someone like me to hell? I don't want to know a God like that!"

She sounded so reasonable. Surely God is fair and will keep things in perspective. He'll recognise that decent people like her aren't in the same category as the really sinful people of the world – the murderers, the paedophiles, the rapists. Sinful people like them belong in hell – not her. God will see that even though she isn't perfect, she's basically good at heart. At least she believed in God – he'd have to appreciate that!

Julia, on the other hand, felt very differently. Tormented by guilt from the things that she'd done, she really felt like a sinner. Despite the passing of time, her sins continued to haunt her. Would she ever find relief from these feelings of guilt? Thinking about God only increased her turmoil. If there is a God, what will he say to me? Is feeling really sorry enough? What if it's not? Better not go there… think about something else…

What would God say to each of them? Wouldn't it be great if they could know for certain!

Perhaps they can know.

The uninvited guest

There's nothing quite like an uninvited guest. They seem to have this remarkable power to make or break your party. A friend of mine invited some friends around to celebrate her birthday. She was having a ball when suddenly, an uninvited guest arrived. He was funny, witty, entertaining… everybody loved him! My friend said later that she may as well have left – it was his party from there on in.

Hers wasn't the first party to be hijacked by a gatecrasher. Two thousand years earlier, a man held a dinner party and invited Jesus. Like my friend's party, it got off to a nice smooth start but was turned upside down by an uninvited guest. It's recorded for us in the Bible in Luke's biography of Jesus.[1]

We read initially:

Now one of the Pharisees invited Jesus to have dinner with him, so he went to the Pharisee's house and reclined at the table.

It all sounds very civilised. We're told the host of the evening was a Pharisee – a Jewish religious official. We find out later in the story that his name is Simon. The Pharisees devoted themselves to applying and obeying God's laws – the most famous of which are the Ten Commandments. In other words, the host of this party was on the 'God Squad'!

No doubt this Pharisee had heard some of the reports that were circulating about Jesus. People were saying, "*A great prophet has arisen among us*" and "*God has visited his people!*"[2] It's not surprising that a Pharisee would be curious about Jesus and invite him around for dinner.

I don't know what you think, but this party is sounding good to me. I wouldn't mind reclining at a table, Roman style, enjoying a meal that someone else had prepared. Plus the conversation's being supplied by none other than Jesus – this famous man that two thousand years later people are still talking about! This is warming up to be a pretty pleasant evening.

Tension at the dinner party

But suddenly, the uninvited guest arrives and the party takes on a whole new dimension! Imagine Hillary Clinton enjoying lunch with some friends in an exclusive restaurant, when all of a sudden, Monica Lewinski walks in. Their eyes meet, Hillary's friends choke on their food, everyone in the restaurant puts down their cutlery and moves to the edge of their seats, waiting to see what's going to happen. Feel the tension? You're there.

> When a woman who had lived a sinful life in that town learned that Jesus was eating at the Pharisee's house, she brought an alabaster jar of perfume, and as she stood behind him at his feet weeping, she began to wet his feet with her tears. Then she wiped them with her hair, kissed them and poured perfume on them.

"… a woman who had lived a sinful life in that town…". The passage doesn't spell out the details of her sin, though it's hard not to hazard a guess. What is clear is that she's a woman with quite a reputation! She's a sinner in the house of a 'saint' – well a moral, upstanding citizen, anyway.

You can just imagine how this Pharisee must be feeling. Not only does he have an uninvited guest to contend with, but look who this gatecrasher is! All eyes are on Jesus to see how he's going to handle this woman – especially the eyes of the host. He sees that this woman presents quite a good little test for Jesus.

> When the Pharisee who had invited him saw this, he said to himself, "If this man were a prophet, he would know who is touching him and what kind of a woman she is – that she's a sinner."

Perhaps you're someone who can really relate to this sinful woman – a bit like my friend, Julia. You may not be a prostitute or a murderer (perhaps you are), but you might know what it's like to feel burdened by guilt, to deeply regret some of the things that you've done. Just like this woman, you might know exactly what it's like to feel like a sinner, and perhaps to be judged by others.

Or perhaps you relate more to Simon, as Dana would. Maybe you believe in God and think of yourself as a good person. Perhaps you try to obey the Ten Commandments. You may even be Jewish. You may not be perfect, but compared to some, you're really pretty good.

A story and a question

Well, for the benefit of both – but particularly those who relate more to Simon – Jesus tells this story:

> Jesus answered him, "Simon, I have something to tell you."
> "Tell me, teacher," he said.
> "Two men owed money to a certain money-lender. One owed him five hundred denarii[3], and the other fifty.[4] Neither of them had the money to pay him back, so he cancelled the debts of both. Now which of them will love

him more?"

Simon replied, "I suppose the one who had the bigger debt cancelled."

"You have judged correctly," Jesus said.

Notice the word 'answered'. Jesus knows exactly what Simon is thinking! He responds by throwing a test of his own back at Simon. It's a fairly provocative little scenario Jesus paints. He seems to be suggesting both the woman and Simon have a debt they can't repay. But surely that can't be right – Simon's a good person, a religious person. He's devoted his life to obeying God's law. He's the last person you'd expect to have a debt – Simon certainly doesn't think he has one. So what's Jesus saying in this little story that he tells?

Well, Jesus doesn't leave Simon wondering. He makes himself crystal clear.

> *Then he turned toward the woman and said to Simon "Do you see this woman? I came into your house. You did not give me any water for my feet, but she wet my feet with her tears and wiped them with her hair.*
>
> *You did not give me a kiss, but this woman from the time I entered, has not stopped kissing my feet. You did not put oil on my head, but she has poured perfume on my feet."*

Simon wasn't looking quite so good anymore! He'd failed to show Jesus basic courtesies. His lack of love stood in vivid contrast to the devotion shown by the woman. Yet if Simon was taken aback by Jesus' observations, the final verdict would have rendered him speechless.

> *"Therefore I tell you, her many sins have been forgiven, for she loved much. But he who has been forgiven little loves little."*

In referring to her many sins, Jesus subtly signalled to Simon that he knew exactly "what kind of a woman" she was – that she was "a sinner". Jesus hadn't failed Simon's test – he'd nailed it. By Simon's reckoning, Jesus must at least have been a prophet – a scary thought for Simon, given what Jesus had been saying. For rather than denouncing the sinful woman, Jesus was condemning him – Simon the Pharisee! Simon's head must have been spinning – his party had entered the surreal! Why would Jesus forgive a sinner and condemn a 'saint'? It seems like judgement in reverse.

The sin debt

Upon reflection, Simon would have found most of the answers in Jesus' story and its conclusion in the two lines above. The nature of the debts had finally become clear. In the same way that the two men needed their debts forgiven, both Simon and the woman needed their sins forgiven. Their debt was their sin – both Simon and the woman had a sin debt.

What was their sin? To spell it out S…I…N: <u>S</u>elf <u>I</u>s <u>N</u>o 1.[5] Rather than treating God as No 1, they made themselves No 1 instead.

The Apostle Paul, who was also a Pharisee, defines sin well. He writes:

No one seeks for God, all have turned aside.[6]

In other words, everyone is guilty of sin. Far from seeking God, all of us have turned away from Him. Even though He made us and the world we live in, we act as if we don't owe God anything. If our lives are a party, we treat God as an uninvited guest. We prefer to ignore him – for we don't like to share the limelight!

My friend Dana serves as a perfect illustration. As we

watched our kids play, I said to her "Given you already believe in God, would you like to get to know God better?" She thought for a moment and then replied, "No, I don't suppose I would".

S…I…N… Self Is No 1.

Well there's a key thing we need to know about our sinful woman at Simon's party. Not only was she a sinner – she admitted it. She was profoundly more aware than Simon, who'd failed to see that underneath all his high moral standards and religious practices, he too had a debt he couldn't pay.

You see, Simon made a very common mistake in his thinking about sin. He made the mistake of comparing himself to other, more sinful people. In comparison, Simon thought he was pretty good. He thought he'd sinned little and had little need for forgiveness. He didn't think he needed Jesus to cancel his debt because he didn't think he had one. However notice that ominous line in Jesus' story – *"Neither had the money to pay him back"*. Even if Simon had sinned *less*, he'd still sinned. He therefore had a debt.

So it's to the woman, not Simon, that Jesus says, *"Your sins are forgiven."*

Jesus was telling her what she already knew. At some point in the past, she had heard about the possibility of forgiveness through faith in Jesus. She may well have heard it from Jesus himself! She'd sinned much; she'd been forgiven much – that's why she loved much. All her feelings of guilt and regret had been finally dealt with. An enormous weight had been lifted from her shoulders, and it all came bubbling out of her on this day as tears of relief, thankfulness and love. And so we find our sinner lovingly caring for the most lowly of Jesus' needs, washing his feet with her tears and pouring perfume on them.

Raising the stakes

In forgiving the woman's sins, Jesus had profoundly raised the stakes – and everyone at the table knew it.

> *Then those who were eating with him began to say among themselves "Who is this, who even forgives sins?"*

That indeed was the question! There was only one who could forgive sins, and that was God. Jesus was either a blasphemer... or God. Which box to put him in was everyone's dilemma. The party began with people wondering whether a prophet had come to town. It ended with them wondering whether God had come around.

As Luke's account of Simon's party draws to a close, Jesus has the final words

> *Jesus said to the woman, "Go in peace, your faith has saved you".*

Notice it's her faith that saved her. Not her love, but her faith in Jesus – her faith that Jesus was God and that he could forgive her sins. So in honesty and humility, she acknowledged her debt and let Jesus deal with it. Yet it was an undertaking that cost him dearly. For to deal with her sin and cancel her debt, Jesus paid it for her. When Jesus died on the cross, he took the punishment she deserved for treating God as an uninvited guest, for making herself No 1. Jesus died in her place so that she might be saved.

Yet while the woman's faith saved her, Simon's faith sealed his fate. He was a man of great faith, he even worshipped God. However rather than putting his faith in Jesus, Simon put his faith in himself. He was confident that his high moral standards and religious practices would save him. Yet ultimately, his faith proved powerless to save. It could not cancel his unpaid debt.

And so this remains a story of triumph and tragedy, a story of salvation and condemnation. For while our sinful woman goes home saved, Simon is left with an unpaid debt.

Who are you in the story?

So to those of us who related more to the sinful woman – what great news this part of the Bible brings! No longer do we need to feel burdened by guilt for the things that we've done, no matter how bad they might be. For when Jesus died on the cross, he took the punishment we deserved for our sin. He died in our place so that we might be forgiven. Just like this sinful woman, we too can have our debt paid for by the blood of Jesus, and love him greatly in return.

To those of us who related more to Simon – we need to take great care! The challenge for us is: will we make Simon's mistake of comparing ourselves to others, while failing to see that we too are guilty of sin (<u>S</u>elf <u>I</u>s <u>N</u>o 1)? Will we recognise that we too have a debt that we can't pay? For Jesus is the only one not guilty of sin, the only one who can pay our debt and save us.

A woman once said to me that she didn't think it was fair that Jesus should pay her debt. She thought she should pay it herself. Perhaps she too had missed that crucial line in Jesus' story: *"Neither had the money to pay him back"*. We cannot pay *off* our debt ourselves, whether it be by good works, giving money, going to the synagogue or church, praying... Simon teaches us that! However someone needs to pay *for* it. Jesus lovingly warns us that on Judgement Day, God will certainly punish those with outstanding debts. Please, consider carefully who'll pay for your sin – Jesus... or you?

Jesus described Heaven as an enormous banquet – the party to end all parties. Who would have dreamed it would be the sinful woman, not Simon, who would be a guest there?

I hope you'll be there; but this I know for certain – there'll be no uninvited guests at that party.

ENDNOTES
1. Luke 7:36-50
2. Luke 7:16
3. A denarius was a labourer's or soldier's daily wage.
4. One owed about one-and-three-quarter years' wages, the other about two months' worth.
5. I'm grateful to Craig Blacket for this explanation.
6. Romans 3:11-12

Relationship

Lesley Ramsay

*M*y friend sat across from me at my kitchen table, her eyes red and swollen. She had lost a lot of weight. It had been six weeks since that stunning revelation which came completely out of the blue: that her husband of 15 years was leaving her because he had fallen in love with a colleague. People had told her she would be better off without him, and that time would heal the hurt. But here she was, in her words, "in a deep black hole, screaming and no-one can hear me".

Relationships in trouble

Statistics now tell us that for the first time in human history, divorce has replaced death as the most common conclusion to marriage. With more than 50% of marriages ending in divorce, you would think that men and women would slip in and out of marriage with barely a thought, and as easily as we change our shoes.

Is the answer to discard marriage as archaic and obsolete, a grand institution that has had its day? Are traditional marriages an endangered species?

But my friend's experience tells us that there is more going on beneath the raw statistics. There is hurt and pain, a sense of betrayal, and a realisation that life has dealt a cruel blow. Those emotions are present because she has loved, and been loved, because she committed herself to this man, and thought that he was committed to her. We won't get rid of the emotions by dispensing with marriage.

Part of what it means to be human is to love, and allow ourselves to be loved. It is bound up in our security as women – to be specially significant to one person.

God and marriage

It may surprise you to know that God invented marriage. In fact God invented sex! We get this picture of God being a cosmic kill-joy. He doesn't want people to enjoy themselves at all, and especially when it comes to sex. But it was his idea. He thought of it first. He gave us our sexuality and our sex drive, and it's his desire that we enjoy this great gift to us men and women. If you were to read that part of the Bible where the first wedding is recorded[1], you would actually pick up this sense of fun and excitement.

It's worth asking, isn't it, why did God invent marriage? God creates two people, a man and a woman, and puts them in a special relationship with each other. Why? The Bible suggests there are three reasons.

The first is *loneliness*. When God created the man, he made the comment, "It is not good for him to be alone". And so he made, not just another man, but a woman! Men and women were made for each other to combat loneliness. Being together was great.

Can you remember when you met a man that you were really attracted to? All you wanted to do was spend as much time with him as possible. When you were apart, you felt kind of empty, but when you were together, nothing else mattered, the rest of the world was not even there, your whole body tingled, the sun shone brighter – no, come to think of it, you didn't even notice if it was sunny or raining! You were with him and that was all that mattered.

When our son was engaged, it never ceased to amaze me how he could come home after being with his fiancée for the whole day, and then as soon as he walked in the door, ring her up and talk for another hour or two. But then I realised I'd forgotten what it was like to be not yet married, and I took for granted being together with the man I loved.

Great relationship, committed sex

The second reason was to provide an opportunity for a *significant personal relationship*. The man and the woman are able to relax in an atmosphere of trust – two people who love each other, who are committed to each other. God's design was for no embarrassment, no bickering, no nagging, no putting the other down. A great relationship.

The third reason was that marriage was the context for *sex*. God says, "They will become one flesh". We live today in a *Sex in the City* kind of world where the sexual act is the common way of relating to the opposite sex.

But at some point, when a woman really loves a man, the sexual act takes on enormous significance – they really do become 'one flesh'. And she is enormously hurt if he breaks that 'one flesh' bond, and goes and forms another 'one flesh' with another woman. She feels betrayed. That is why, built into the idea is the sense of commitment to each other. Because we are 'one flesh', we're committed to each other – come what may.

I heard a cynic say one day that marriage was a legally sanctioned opportunity for two people to destroy each other. But there's no hint of that in this first marriage. Delighted to be in each other's company, a great relationship where they supported and loved each other perfectly, a commitment to each other and no one else, unembarrassed, satisfying and great sex! This is marriage as it was intended to be. And why did God create it like this? Because, deep down inside, this is what we desire, what we crave for.

We hate being lonely. We love the companionship of like–minded people that we love being with, and who want to spend time with us. We desperately desire relationships that are mutually satisfying and not tainted with tension or difficulty. We crave the sense that one man would be totally and exclusively committed to us, and no-one else, and that that exclusive commitment would be expressed in a sexual relationship. That's what I want – I suspect that's what most people want. And that's what God gave to his creation when he gave them marriage.

It's all gone wrong

But as I intimated at the beginning, it's clear that something has gone horribly wrong. We're a long way from that picture at the beginning of the Bible. One in two marriages are irreversibly broken. Couples now live more and more in trial marriage relationships before they commit in a permanent way – but these inevitably end in divorce also.

Husbands and wives don't delight in each other's company. They live lonely lives in the midst of a marriage… A ten-year-old was once asked for a definition of 'isolation'. She replied, "that's when someone excludes you". Husbands excluding wives and wives excluding husbands results in loneliness – a sense of nothing.

You can share a bed, eat at the same dinner table, watch the same TV, share the same bank account, parent the same children – and still be alone. You may have sex, but you don't love each other. You may talk, but you don't communicate. You may live together, but you don't share life with one another.

That's what it's like for John and Jenny. They've been married for fifteen years. Both work at demanding jobs, and after Jenny has picked up the kids from After-School Care, and they've managed take-away in front of the TV, the only energy that's left is consumed by washing, ironing, dishes, and bathing the kids. When John and Jenny finally crawl into bed at night, they've got nothing to say to each other and they fall asleep facing in opposite directions.

The reason why

Why are we like this? How did we get here? The Bible tells us that it's because we as humans have chosen to ignore and sideline God, and the result is imperfect life and difficult marriages. Our self-centred absorption with our own needs and happiness means that we inevitably hurt those closest to us, those we have promised to love and care for to the death.

Ponder this question: Have you ever known of a divorce, the breakup of a marriage, that has been a happy experience for the couple involved? I never have. Adultery, marriage breakdown, divorce – they all hurt! Sometimes, one more than the other, but it always hurts. In the movie *Random Hearts,* the character played by Harrison Ford loses his wife in an airline crash. As he mourns her death, he discovers that she was having an adulterous affair, and this knowledge completely unbalances him.

Often it hurts other people. When Kurt Cobain, the grunge rock star, committed suicide in the 90's, reporters digging into his background discovered that his parents had divorced when he was eight. His mother said that he had been profoundly affected by the experience – so much so that at an earlier suicide attempt, he had a note in his pocket that said, "I'd rather die than go through a divorce." Why?

Because we were not intended to break up. God knew that the best environment for a 'one flesh' relationship was a faithful, lifelong commitment between a husband and wife. And anything that breaks that bond hurts.

Divorcing God

There's a little sentence tucked away in the Bible that goes like this: *"The Lord God of Israel says, 'I hate divorce'."* [2] One of the reasons that he hates it is because he knows how much it hurts his people. If you have ever experienced divorce, be assured that God knows how much that hurt you – and he hates it! There's another reason. He's not just on the outside looking in. He knows how much divorce hurts, because he's been through it.

Read what a man named Jeremiah wrote:

Have you seen what faithless Israel has done? She has gone up on every high hill and under every spreading tree and has committed adultery there. I thought that after she had done all this she would return to me, but she did not... I gave faithless Israel her certificate of divorce and sent her away because of all her adulteries... Because Israel's immorality mattered so little to her, she defiled the land and committed adultery with stone and wood.

Go, proclaim this message towards the north:

"Return faithless Israel" declares the LORD, "I will frown on you no longer, for I am merciful" declares the LORD, "I will not be angry forever. Only acknowledge your guilt – you have rebelled against the LORD your God. You have scattered your favours to foreign gods under every spread-ing tree, and have not obeyed me," declares the LORD.

"Return, faithless people," declares the LORD, "for I am your husband." [3]

Here, God is speaking to his people. The relationship that he has with his creation is so personal and intimate that he compares it to a marriage. He is the husband, and we – his creation, his people that he loves – are his wife.

This wife has been unfaithful and committed adultery. How have we done that? By turning our backs on God.

In Jeremiah's day, they worshipped other gods of wood and stone. We are much more sophisticated. We just ignore him and think that we can get on and live our lives very well without him, thank you very much. But the effect is the same. He's marginalised, shut out, put over in the corner. Meanwhile, we pursue with passion the things that we really love – our own identity, our self-esteem, a career, our relationships, our desire to control our own destiny.

We have been grossly unfaithful to God. It's like we have gone after another bloke! We want to divorce God. We've told him, "I don't need you anymore. I've found someone much more attractive. I want you out of my life." We don't use those words, but that's what we do.

God's ultimate act of love

The interesting thing, though, is God's response to the way we have treated him. When a husband or wife discovers that their partner is committing adultery, their response is usually shock, disappointment, a loss of trust, maybe a willingness to give them another chance and take them back. But if the betrayal and the adultery happen again and again, trust totally disappears and the relationship is irretrievably broken.

But God never gives up on his adulterous wife. He wants her to give up the adultery and return to him so that he can be merciful and forgiving. Unlike our human partners he never stops loving, never stops pursuing us, never stops having compassion on us.

And we know that because one day he had to deal with our betrayal once and for all, and make it possible for us to be faithful. The death of his son, Jesus, on a cross in Jerusalem two thousand years ago was God saying "My adulterous wife, my unfaithful people, I love you so passionately that I am willing to give my only son to die for you." And so Jesus was nailed to a cross, because we had been unfaithful. That's what God, the 'husband', does for his 'wife'. A husband like that is hard to find.

Entering into relationship with God

After a spate of high profile marriage break-ups recently, the editor of a women's magazine wrote:

> *"Couples are breaking up all around us. Friends, families, celebrities.... It's getting scary. My husband and I keep repeating a mantra, "Be nice to each other, be nice to each other." It seems so obvious, but sometimes it can be really tough. When you are feeling tired and grumpy it's all too easy to take it out on your partner."*[4]

Working hard at our marriage is a hard slog, but essential. Being nice to each other is..... well, nice. But it's going to take a lot more than that to have a marriage that doesn't just survive, but nurtures both partners – in which both man and woman know they are safe and significant and loved and appreciated and accepted.

Getting right with God is tough too. With God, we want to do our own thing. We don't like giving up our independence to another person, even if it is God. But we must, otherwise we'll be left out in the cold, and end up alone – very alone. That's what happens to people who keep on rejecting God over and over again. Finally God says, "OK, I'll leave you alone, for eternity." The alternative is that we say "Yes, God – I want to accept Jesus' death for me. I want you to forgive me. I want to enter into a secure, loving relationship with you…"

When we get to the end of the Bible, we find a lovely picture of a wedding reception. The wedding is between the groom – God – and the bride – his people who have returned to him. It's a picture of heaven, and it will be a great and joyous time. Will you be there – part of that great marriage celebration, forever secure in your relationship with God?

Or will you be on your own, all alone?

ENDNOTES
1. Genesis 2:18-24
2. Malachi 2:16
3. Jeremiah 3:6-9, 12-14
4. Alana House, Editor. *Womans Day,* January 31, 2005

Lauren and Rod's story

Lauren and Rod are married with four energetic children. They became Christians 14 years ago. In the following interview, they talk about that pivotal point of their lives.

~

Lauren, tell me a bit about your early childhood. Did you have much to do with God then?

Lauren: I had no church upbringing to speak of. I have a vague memory of going to Sunday School for a few months when I was about 4, but then we moved, and I never went again. The only time I heard Jesus' name was when someone in the family was swearing.

Did you ever have RE at school?

Lauren: Only the odd occasion when I went with friends to their scripture class, but never consistently or for long periods. Yet all during that time, I felt as if a god was there. I remember when I was in trouble as a teenager, I would pray to Mary or anybody else I could think of. I didn't have a clue who I was praying to.

As if you had a sense that somebody was out there and they were bigger than you were?

Lauren: I felt sure somebody was there, I just didn't know anything about him or her. I suppose I'd just hoped that they were good. When Rod and I started going out together, things hadn't changed. We never really talked about God.

After we'd been going out together for a couple of years, Rod's sister – who had become a Christian earlier – started trying to 'witness' to us. She annoyed the hell out of me. She kept trying to tell us how to live, and to add insult to injury, when we'd go to stay with her, she wouldn't let us sleep together. I just didn't want to know about it.

What about you, Rod? What were your early thoughts about God?
Rod: My parents were not church-goers, but they sent me off to Sunday school as a young kid so I could "make up my own mind about religion." For many years I hung around the church scene, went to Sunday school, God Squad and CEBS (Church of England Boys' Society). But in my teenage years I stopped going.

Did your Mum and Dad talk to you much about God?
Rod: No. My father was anti-church. He had his own version of *Jesus Loves Me, This I Know.* It went "Jesus loves me, I don't think", and he would often sing it to us.

Did your mother get upset about that?
Rod: No, not really – it was just one more thing about Dad that annoyed Mum. Besides, in the end, Mum followed Dad. I think Dad believed in God, but it would have been contrary to the mindset of the day to talk about God.

So what did all this mean for you, Rod?
Rod: Well, as I said, I had lots of exposure to church groups, but I never owned it for myself. Unlike Lauren, I believed that the God of the Bible was there. I even talked to him. But once I'd reached my teens I had lost contact with church and church people.

Who was this sister who became a Christian?

Rod: That was my second eldest sister, Debbie. She is married to Jack, who at the time had a heroin problem. By chance (or design) he'd ended up at a dry-out centre near to us, and while he was there he became a Christian. His conversion story was bizarre – all these weird supernatural things happened to him. A little later, Debbie became a Christian too, but their stories were so strange and their lives so changed that I thought Christians were nuts.

Yet I couldn't deny what God had done in their lives, or what they were saying. They were full on, living for Jesus. The problem was that they'd started making life difficult for us. When Lauren and I went to stay with them, Deb wouldn't let us sleep together. This seemed ludicrous because we had been dating for a good two years.

How did you feel about that, Lauren?

Lauren: I hated it. I used to call her "Rod's nutty Christian sister". I didn't think she had a right to do that to us, but while we were under her roof, we had to obey her rules. After dinner, though, when the Christian talk would begin, that was it for me. I would leave and go up to my room – I didn't want to know about it. Most of all, I hated the fact that Rod would stay up late and talk to Jack and Debbie, while I was alone in my room.

So what did you talk about with your sister, Rod?

Rod: It was a strange sensation. It was compelling, but on the other hand I didn't want to hear it either. I knew if I listened long enough I'd have to do something about it. We'd come away from those trips with Lauren saying, "Who does she think she is?" and "Thank goodness we're out of there", but I knew there was a lot of truth in what they were saying about God. I knew God wouldn't be pleased with the way we were living.

Lauren: That didn't bother me. I thought I was OK. But Rod used to try and scare me with stories from the Bible.

What sort of stories?
Rod: The favourite stories of the non-Christian – seven-headed monsters, angels with trumpets, red dragons… Particularly where it said that there'd be a reckoning, and we'd be answerable for what we'd done.

Did that frighten you?
Rod: It would frighten anyone, wouldn't it? It wasn't the seven-headed monsters that were really scary. It was the fact that God was coming back, and what were we going to do about it? So you see, there would be these spikes in life when I would get scared and think about God. And then I'd put it all to one side and forget about it – we'll worry about it later.

And you never gave much thought to these things in your teenage years, Lauren?
Lauren: Not at all! I was a really wild child. Mum and Dad literally didn't know what to do with me. Mum had led a very restricted life, and they thought the best method of child-rearing was to do the exact opposite and just let me do what I wanted. And I did!

From about twelve I was getting into all sorts of trouble, including drugs and drinking, staying out all night with my friends. I'd finished Year Ten and started working at 15. Even though I wasn't old enough, I'd spend all Friday night at the pub, come home about 5.00 am, and then go to work at 7:30, still hung over from the night before.

How old were you when you met Rod?

Lauren: I was 16. Because of the way I had been brought up, I was insecure. I wanted security above all else. I was looking for someone who would treat me decently, and Rod was nice. I liked what I'd found, and I wanted to hang onto it.

Rod: As for me, I had a great circle of friends. Then along came Lauren. I loved her too, but I wanted her to be like one of my mates.

Lauren: Rod wanted the best of both worlds – his mates and me. But I didn't want to share him. I wanted him all to myself. I was selfish – and angry, too. Angry at the world, or at God – at men in general. It meant there was always an underlying mistrust of Rod. I always felt as if he was going to pull the rug out from underneath me.

How did you react to this, Rod?

Rod: My underlying philosophy was "I'll do right by you if you do right by me". But it couldn't work because of Lauren's insecurity. She wanted proof all the time that everything was OK. I couldn't sustain that sort of relationship. I felt trapped, and actually tried to end the relationship several times. But we always ended up getting back together again.

The turning point came after we'd been going out for three years. Lauren was 19 and I was 23. Lauren told me one day she was pregnant. We were both in shock, but Lauren had always said that if this happened, we should terminate the pregnancy. I agreed.

Lauren: My mother rang up and organised the whole thing. I asked her if I would be conscious during the procedure, and she thought that I would be. I started having second thoughts. Then I talked to my boss at work, and she urged me to carefully consider what I was doing, reminding me that this was no 'flash in the pan' baby, but one that had been conceived out of love. I went through an agonising time, but finally became convinced I wanted to keep the baby, even if it meant doing it on my own.

~

Rod, were you aware of what Lauren was going through?
Rod: I had no idea. When she told me she was not going through with the abortion, I was shocked – and frightened! This was a big thing. I'd avoided responsibility all my life, and now I was going to have to be responsible. I was also very angry with her. This change of mind had seemed so sudden and she hadn't talked to me about it. When I look back on it, my parents and my upbringing saved me. They would have expected me to do the right thing. I also now see it was a great blessing from God. If we had gone through with the abortion, I would be a different person now. Much meaner, I'm sure.

Lauren: We had no money between us, so about six weeks before the baby was due, we moved into a room in my parents' house. It was an awful time – I don't know how we got through it. Erin was born and we settled into parenthood. It was terrible. Rod had a new job, which he loved, and I was stuck at home with a new baby, no life and no friends – totally isolated. I was so desperate that I started ringing help lines for someone to talk to.

Rod: It was during this time that our consciences started worrying us. Parenthood reinforced our uneasiness about living together – having this baby and not being married. It just didn't feel right.

Lauren: Initially, the pressure to get married came from Rod's family. My parents really didn't care. As we talked about it, Rod said we ought to go to church and talk to a minister about it. I had a problem with that. Wasn't the church just some place where people put their own interpretation on God? I didn't want to have to do anything that they said. But at the end of the day, Rod felt we had to get married to please God. After a lot of discussion, I gave in and we ended up at a church.

Rod: Even though we wanted to talk about getting married, we couldn't bring ourselves to talk to the minister. We used to try and be as unobtrusive as possible and then leave as quickly as we could when church had finished. About the third time we were there, one of the ministers collared us and introduced himself. We agreed to meet with him.

Lauren: The minister's name was Rick and he offered to do a series of six Bible Studies with us called *Christianity Explained*. The first three studies were about Jesus, and I just soaked it up like a sponge. I understood for the first time that I was not a descendant of an ape. I had always thought that coming from a monkey was so humiliating. My life before had been so cruddy that now, to know that God had a purpose for me – that I was part of his plan – turned me upside down!

I wanted to become a Christian then and there, but I was too scared to say anything. After the third study, though, I couldn't contain myself any longer. I told Rick, "I want to do this now". He helped me to talk to God. So I prayed, asking God to forgive me for my sin and to take control of my life. And he did.

~

What about you Rod? Were you convinced in the same way Lauren was?
Rod: No, it was very different for me. I understood what Jesus had done for me but felt that I had to feel differently

than I did, or that I would need to clean up my act more before God would accept me. To simply make a logical choice on the basis of facts was too easy. I failed to understand that God was saying to me, "Come as you are, and we'll sort out your life as we go." To compound the problem, here was my fiancé who knew literally nothing, and she had become a Christian. To make matters worse, this minister was too 'in my face'. He wouldn't let me get away with anything; this guy was hammering me. I knew what Jesus had done for me, so why wasn't I taking God seriously?

The straw that broke the camel's back was when he told Lauren that now she was a Christian, all her relationships had to come under God's microscope – and that included me! I was sitting at the same table. What do you say to something like that? Rick left, and I went out on my own. Thinking about Lauren and Rick wasn't helping; I had to settle this thing between God and me. I took a ball and went to an oval, and over the next couple of hours, thrashed things around in my mind.

Finally I gave in and said to God, "Father, I understand what you did for me. I'm now yours. I want to follow you from now on. I'll leave you to make the changes as you see fit"… Still no miracle. It was all very ordinary. The changes were to come later, and I came to understand that the blessings of coming to know him were better than any flash-in-the-pan miracle.

Lauren: So we became Christians on the same day – me in the morning, Rod in the afternoon. We knew things in our lives had to change. We stopped smoking drugs, we smashed all our drug smoking implements and we laid off the booze. I was collecting the unmarried mothers' benefit. I knew it was wrong and I had to own up to Social Security. I didn't want to give it up – I couldn't see how we could survive without it. All we had to our name was a car. I remember saying to God, "It's only because of you that I'm doing this".

Rod: But we survived. We learnt God always provides. Abundantly.

The real test was when we decided to stop sleeping together till our wedding. Rick urged us to get married straight away, but we wanted to save up and have the traditional 'do'. Remember, we had a child, and there was nowhere else in the house to go. That meant sleeping in the same bed for nine months without…

Did you ever feel cheated? Ever feel like you had been pushed into a corner?
Rod: No. It was extremely hard, but God had blessed us and we knew he was looking after us. We wanted to honour God.

～

Lauren, what was it about Jesus that impressed you?
Lauren: He said that his purpose in coming to earth was to die for me. I'd not known who Jesus was before, and he seemed almost too good to be true. All the things I'd yearned for in life – comfort and security – I saw in Jesus. Rod could offer me these things in part, but he was bound to let me down. My expectations were high and he wasn't perfect. But Jesus was a different matter. He was perfect and I knew he would never let me down, no matter what.

Rod: The big thing that I understood for the first time was that God wanted me to come just as I was. I always thought that I needed to get to a certain level before he would accept me. I completely missed that Jesus had paid the price for my stupidity, all the dumb things I'd done, all the time I'd wasted. He wasn't saying, "Clean up your act and then come to me." Rather, he was saying, "Come now. I'll clean you up. I'll change you."

Lauren: And he has changed us. We are very different people now to the people we were fourteen years ago. We are much softer, kinder people – much more outgoing. He has made a big difference.

Rod: He has taught me to forgive – to say sorry, without qualification – to Lauren, to the kids when I've failed them, to people at work…

Do you have any regrets about becoming Christians?
Rod: None. Knowing that all that has gone before you in life has been forgiven and forgotten because of Jesus' death is so liberating and comforting. God has given me a fresh start, a chance to start all over again. Why would we want to go back to our old way of life? It was a miserable existence compared with what we have now. We threw everything out and replaced it with Jesus. We ran with him, and it's been better than anything we could have imagined.

There's a part in the Bible where Jesus asks his disciples if they want to desert him. One of them replies, *"Lord, to whom shall we go? You alone have the words of eternal life."*[1] That's exactly how we feel. Where else could we go?

ENDNOTE
1. John 6:68-69

Compassion
Michelle Underwood

I'm a woman in my early thirties, but already I am aware that people suffer enormously. Everyone experiences pain or tragedy at some time.

Women struggle and suffer in all manner of ways. It might be period pain or PMT or the pains of childbirth. Perhaps it is discrimination in the workplace, or domestic violence or sexual abuse. Many women suffer from post-natal depression, breast cancer, or infertility. Others know the strains of motherhood, a bad marriage, or what it is like to grieve over the death of a child. As Madonna laments in one of her popular songs, *"Do you know what it feels like in this world for a girl?"*

Often we just long to have someone understand – 'to know what it feels like'. To give us a hug, a home cooked meal, an expression of compassion… There is nothing worse when you are suffering than to have people say nothing. Suffering is difficult; suffering alone is unbearable.

God and suffering

Have you ever wondered what God thinks about our suffering? Does he know what's going on? Does he care? Or are we all alone in this world of pain?

When Jesus was on earth he met a lot of women who were suffering – women who were sick, poor, discriminated against, outcast. This is the story of one woman who was suffering and her encounter with Jesus. It's also a story that teaches us a lot about the suffering world we live in, and what God thinks about it.

> *Soon afterward, Jesus went to a town called Nain, and his disciples and a large crowd went along with him. As he approached the town gate, a dead person was being carried out – the only son of his mother, and she was a widow. And a large crowd from the town was with her.*
>
> *When the Lord saw her, his heart went out to her and he said, "Don't cry."*
>
> *Then he went up and touched the coffin, and those carrying it stood still. He said, "Young man, I say to you, get up!" The dead man sat up and began to talk, and Jesus gave him back to his mother.*
>
> *They were all filled with awe and praised God. "A great prophet has appeared among us," they said. 'God has come to help his people." This news about Jesus spread throughout Judea and the surrounding country.1*

In this story, Jesus and a crowd of followers approach a Middle Eastern township. As they draw near the town gate, they see another crowd of people coming toward them. Moving closer, it becomes clearer exactly why this crowd is gathered – it is a funeral procession. The coffin is held up in front, being carried out for burial. The mourners follow behind, crying and wailing. It is an especially sad funeral – the funeral of a young man.

I don't know if you've ever been to the funeral of a young person before. There's something particularly tragic about someone being 'cut off' in the prime of their life. There's a real sense that 'this is not the way it is supposed to be'. People should live long and happy lives. People shouldn't die young.

Why did my son die?

As the story unfolds, the picture becomes more heart-wrenching. We gradually find out more about the one for whom the grief is no doubt most intense – the young man's mother. She has lost her *only* beloved son. It is hard to imagine the depth of her sorrow.

The story then tells us that not only has she lost her only son, but she had previously lost her husband too. She is a widow. What desolation she would be feeling – first her husband, now her only son. And in those days, to be a woman without family was devastating. Without husband or son she would have no form of income, and would be facing a future of destitution and begging. When Jesus walks into this town and meets this woman, he walks into a scene of immense pain.

It's a little microcosm of life in this world, really. This world we live in can be a hard place, full of pain and tragedy. On the one hand this world is overflowing with beautiful and amazing things – like relationships, families and loved ones. Yet on the other hand, it is marred by pain and death. Children die. Husbands die. Others are left to grieve.

Why is the world like this? 'Why,' this woman may have asked, 'do people die?' Have you ever asked these kinds of questions?

A world gone wrong

The Bible is clear that God didn't make the world like this. The world is not as it is supposed to be. Pain and suffering and death are part of a world gone wrong.

What has happened, the Bible explains, is that people have turned their backs on God. They live life their own way, without regard for him or the way he would want us to live.

So much of the suffering in this world is a direct result of people ignoring God and not living his way. Murder, rape, abuse, lies, greed, selfishness and injustice are just a few examples of the way in which human beings have turned their backs on God, and suffering is the result for them, and for others. In our own way, we are all part of the problem.

God is rightly angry at people's rejection of him, and has declared the just punishment. That punishment is death and being cut off from him and his gift of life forever. All of us now live in a world that is ruined. Our relationship with God is broken and we are under the shadow of judgement and death. And there is nothing we can do to fix it. Life now is hard, and suffering is an everyday reality of living in a world that is not how it was designed to be.

So this woman's suffering is not necessarily a direct consequence of her treatment of God – we actually know nothing about her. We don't know if she was particularly moral, or immoral, religious, or anything. Her painful experience, like so many others, is the tragic result of just being a part of this world gone wrong.

The light in the darkness

Does that mean God no longer cares for us? Has he abandoned the world and left it to run its own miserable course? Is there any future hope? What present comfort is available? We need to go back and examine Jesus to find the answers to such questions.

On seeing this funeral procession and the woman's grief, look at Jesus' reaction:

When the Lord saw her, his heart went out to her and he said, "Don't cry"

His heart goes out to her – he really aches for her and her grief. The woman doesn't say anything to him. She doesn't approach him or ask him for anything – Jesus simply sees her and her situation and is deeply moved. He is not cold or stand-offish. He doesn't just stand back and let her go by without saying a word. He feels for her, reaches out to her and speaks tender words of comfort. In Jesus' words we hear the sympathy of God. God is not cold and uncaring and distant. He is gentle and kind, understanding and good. God does care; he has come into this world in the person of Jesus and he says, "Don't cry."

Now often when people say "Don't cry" they mean "Be brave. Pull yourself together. There's nothing you can do about this so crying is not going to help." After all, there's nothing we can do about death. Even mothers – who always seem to be the ones able to fix any situation – even they are powerless in the face of death. This mother certainly is.

But when Jesus says to the woman "Don't cry" he's not saying "just be brave". He says "Don't cry" because he is going to give her a reason to stop crying. Look at what happens next:

Then he went up and touched the coffin, and those carrying it stood still. He said,

"Young man, I say to you, get up!" The dead man sat up and began to talk, and Jesus gave him back to his mother.

Jesus repels death

With the touch of his hand and a command from his lips, Jesus brings her son back to life. And not just half-heartedly, as though just stirring someone out of a coma. This young man immediately sits up and talks!

What follows is a beautiful picture of reunion as Jesus

gives the young man back to his mother – for it was for her sake that he did this. Jesus saw her, had compassion on her and gave her son back to her.

This is incredible when you think about it. Here is someone who has power to raise people from the dead. This is someone who has compassion on the suffering and the ability to do something about it. Surely, here is someone who has the power to solve the problems of this suffering world!

Could you imagine what it would have been like to witness this? To be in the middle of a funeral and for someone to go up to the coffin, speak to the dead person and tell them to get up, and they do? See how the crowd, who were there, responded:

> *They were all filled with awe and praised God. "A great prophet has appeared among us," they said. "God has come to help his people."*

In Jesus Christ, God has indeed 'come to help his people'. Jesus Christ is the one who is able to fix this broken world. When Jesus raised this young man from the dead, he showed us what life was meant to be like – a world where there is no death or sickness or grief or pain. He gave us a taste, if you like, of the things that he has promised will come. He gave us a glimpse of what life will be like when he returns to make all things new.

Surprisingly, we see here that the Bible portrays Jesus not just as an inspiring man or a good moral teacher, but as divine – God himself, who came to earth and lived as one of us, as a human being. When we read Jesus' words in the Bible, we read God's words. When we see Jesus act, we see God act. When Jesus brings this young man back to life we see God's life-giving power. When we see Jesus' loving treatment of this woman, we see God's compassion on our suffering world.

Compassion for us

Just as Jesus had compassion on this woman, Jesus has compassion on our situation. He knows what it is like to live in
a world under the shadow of death. He knows first-hand
what it is like to suffer. And through his own suffering and
death he has done something to fix our situation. He has provided a way of restoring our ruined relationship with God.

What Jesus did was to come to earth to die, taking God's
punishment for us when he died. He endured all of God's
anger at our rebellion, so that we could be freed and forgiven.
Jesus, in his compassion for us, gave up his life, so that we
could be reconciled to God again, free from the shadow of
judgement.

What is more, just as he raised the young man in this story
to life, so too Jesus was resurrected from death, never to die
again. He is alive now in heaven, compassionate and able to
help all who call on him. What a comfort it is to call on a God
who has himself experienced what it is like to live in this suffering world, and who is far more powerful than death!

That does not mean an end to our physical death and suffering yet – we still live in this old, corrupted world. But
Jesus does promise that those who trust in him can look forward to a day when this world will end. On that day, Jesus
will raise his followers to life again, never to die again. With
new, everlasting bodies they will enjoy life with God in a new
world, where there will be no more suffering, death or pain.
That's what followers of Jesus long for. The only reason it
hasn't happened yet is that God, in his compassion, is waiting for people to turn back to him – to trust in Jesus and
accept the forgiveness and eternal life he offers.

We may not have all the answers to the problems of this
world, but we can know that the Creator of this world cares

for us, has compassion on us, and can be our comfort now if we turn to him and trust in his promises of a new, perfect world to come.

This is a wonderful source of hope. God is not cold, aloof and distant – he is close and kind, gentle and good. Those of you who suffer, look to Jesus and see in him the tender-hearted, compassionate God.

ENDNOTE
1. Luke 7:11-17

Truth
Claire Smith

There are lots and lots of trendy coffee shops where I live, where plenty of trendy people sit outside in the sun, sipping café latte and eating something delicious from the menu. It's what you'd call a café society. In fact, every morning I pass one café where the road workers in their fluorescent safety vests sit in the sun sipping their lattes. Where I live, everyone's into coffee shops – even the men!

Choices, choices

I don't know about you, but I reckon at coffee shops it's easy to spend more time choosing what you're going to eat than actually eating it! You sit there and read the menu, and it all sounds so delicious, then the waitress turns up to take your order and you still can't decide. So you send her away and try to make a decision between the 20 or so things on the menu in front of you.

But the problem is, they all seem so enticing. They're all elaborate and exotic and cooked by someone else. The question is what to pick when it's all just so good?

Of course, the waitress always comes back too soon, and you either have to send her away again, and risk her never returning (because the place is starting to get busy), or just wave your finger over the menu and pick the first thing your finger lands on.

The truth of the matter is we'd probably enjoy eating any

of them and that's why the choice is so hard. Let's face it, if the aim of the exercise was simply to fill the gap in our stomachs, anything (even dry bread) would do the job.

If our only purpose was to stop being hungry, as long as we ate *something*, we'd have done the job.

Pop psychology and the spiritual hole

Now there's a similar sort of thinking that's around today about religion. I think it comes from pop-psychology, which sees our lives as consisting of various compartments – like work, leisure, relationships, exercise and so on – and one of those boxes is religion, or spirituality.

This kind of thinking says that to be a well-balanced and fulfilled person, we have to look after each separate compartment. You need a bit of exercise. You need a bit of leisure, a bit of culture and a bit (not too much) work. And you need to develop your spiritual side, although it doesn't actually matter what you believe so long as you believe something.

It's like there's this spiritual hole in each of us and it doesn't matter *how* we fill it, so long as we do. Just as there's a long menu at the coffee shop to choose from, there's a smorgasbord of religions which we're told will satisfy our spiritual hunger. All we have to do is pick which one we want to fill up on.

It's the experience of believing that counts, not the content of that belief. It doesn't matter what we believe in, so long as we believe something.

Believing the wrong thing

But is that right? Is spiritual hunger like physical hunger? Is belief purely a matter of taste? Can belief, even sincere belief, ever be mistaken?

When I was growing up, one of my friends had a tragic thing happen to his family when we were in high school. His younger brother was playing at a friend's house. His friend had a rifle which he believed – sincerely believed – was empty. He pointed it at my friend's brother – and of course, we all know the dreadful outcome. The gun wasn't empty and my friend's brother was killed with a single shot to the head.

Now, this is a tragic and shocking story. But you see, it's possible to believe something sincerely and be sincerely wrong, and for that wrong belief to have serious and irretrievable consequences. Believing the gun was empty was simply *not enough* because it wasn't *true*.

In complete contrast to the popular saying 'it doesn't matter what you believe so long as you believe something,' it is possible to believe the wrong thing. Believing something is not enough. We must believe the *right* thing.

Being politically incorrect

There's a story in the Bible from the early years of the Christian church in the first century where the Jewish religious rulers are asking two Christian leaders to explain some healings they have been doing.

The authorities want to know 'how and why' they have been performing these miracles. The two Christians, Peter and John, declare it is because of Jesus Christ, who'd been killed by the Roman and Jewish authorities and had been raised from the dead by God.

Then Peter says:

> "Salvation is found in no-one else, for there is no other name under heaven given to men by which we must be saved."[1]

Now this is a bold claim that was as offensive then as it is to today's culture. And if we were to finish reading this account in the Bible, we'd find that the authorities were so outraged and offended and stumped by it that they tried to force Peter and John to stop saying such things and even considered throwing them in gaol.

But let's look at what these two men are saying. They are saying that of all the religions that are around (and of course, there was as many religions around in the first century as there are today), there is really only one that works.

It's a bold claim and even, some may think, an arrogant claim. In our day, it certainly isn't politically correct.

These men are saying that only one religion does the job. That only one religion is true. And that one is belief in Jesus.

But what do they mean and how do they know?

Salvation from the inevitable

Salvation is one of those words that gets thrown around these days without ever really meaning all that much. It seems we all want to be saved from something. For some of us it's boredom or loneliness. For others it's debt or disease or hunger or bankruptcy, or a loveless marriage. Whatever it is for you, we all long to be saved from something.

These are the problems that dominate our lives, the things from which we long to be rescued, the things we hope to escape. But of course, as bad as these things might seem, and in reality might be, they are not our biggest problem. Our biggest problem – the one from which not one of us can escape – is death.

However we might cheat death in this life, the end is inevitable. We love watching rescues on TV – the drama of swimmers being lifted out of the sea, or people being rescued from the housetops of the flood ruined Boscastle. But even for those who seem to have cheated death at the eleventh hour, their twelfth hour will come.

We will all die, and if there is anything we all need salvation from, it is this. We are all powerless in the face of the inevitable.

Death – we only have ourselves to blame

The Bible tells us that the reason for this is that we have each earned death by the way we've lived. Death is the fitting conclusion to our lives.

But why?

The Bible explains that God made us, and he made us to live in love and harmony and obedience to him and at peace with our fellow humans. Had we chosen to live his way, death would not await us.

But each one of us has chosen not to live God's way. We have ignored him. We have disregarded, disrespected and disobeyed him. Some of us have done this consciously and even obviously, but for most of us, our rebellion has looked more like neglect than anything.

We see the consequences of our rejection and disobedience to God all around us, every day. We know the broken relationships. We know the words spoken in anger. We know the pride and bitterness and pain that hide in each of our hearts, even if we only catch a glimpse of it in moments that seem beyond our control.

God sees it too, and his judgement is that because of it, each one of us deserves to die. This is the only appropriate punishment. This judgement is inevitable and inescapable. There is no way to make an eleventh hour escape.

No way, that is, except through Jesus. He is our only means of escape.

This part of the Bible tells us there is no other way – no other person, no other name, no religion, no belief, nothing else – but Jesus. If we look for salvation – and we should be looking – we will be making a fatal mistake if we look anywhere else. It is Jesus or no-one.

How Jesus saves

But how does Jesus save us?

I mentioned earlier that Peter and John in our story explained that Jesus had been killed by the authorities and then raised to life again by God. And this is exactly how Jesus saves us.

You see, when Jesus died on the cross, he took the punishment we deserve. We deserve to die, he did not. But he did die. He chose to die. He loved us so much that he stepped in and took our place. He suffered the death we deserve and paid the debt we ought to pay so that God can forgive us.

That's why there is only one way to be saved. That's why salvation can only be found in one person, because only one person has died a death he didn't deserve and made forgiveness possible. We know he is that one person because he rose from the dead and overcame death.

There's no point in believing meditation or self-improvement will be enough. There's no point in hoping positive thinking, crystals, astrology or saving the environment, or even our own interpretation of Christianity will get us through. They will not be enough.

They can't save us, because without Jesus there is no salvation. Without him there is no escape from the eternal judgement we deserve.

God himself has said there is only one person who can save us, and that person is Jesus. Since we'll all have to answer to God one day, we need to listen to what he says.

There is no point in believing in anything or anyone else, because only Jesus can give us the love and forgiveness that meet our greatest need. He loves us and has died for us so that we might be rescued from death at the eleventh hour. What a remarkable escape!

Belief can be deadly

The sad truth is that life is not like a coffee shop. It matters what we choose – it matters what we believe.

You see, like the tragic story about my friend's brother, it's possible to believe the wrong thing with absolutely deadly consequences because sincerity is not enough when what you're believing is not true.

If you're in a burning building and you mistake the toilet door for the fire escape, you won't wish you'd believed more strongly that the toilet door was the fire escape. You'll regret you believed the wrong thing!

And that's what it's like with Jesus. Each one of us has a choice about what we believe and it's possible to believe the wrong thing. We're each given a choice.

Do we see the world the way God sees it or not? Do we believe in Jesus or not? The consequences of this choice are as simple and final as life and death itself.

We can choose to believe in something other than Jesus, but the consequences are deadly, eternal and inescapable.

Or we can choose God's way.

We can turn to God and trust in Jesus as the only way to be saved from the death and judgement we deserve. From that moment on, we can experience God's forgiveness and love in our daily lives, and look forward to eternity with God.

Sure, death still comes to us, but it is only a passing

moment that serves as the gateway to eternal paradise with God. Believing in Jesus makes a difference now and forever.

The belief 'it doesn't matter what you believe so long as you believe in something' is actually a deadly lie.

It is not enough to believe in *something*. We must believe the truth, and the truth is *Jesus*.

ENDNOTE
1. Acts 4:12

The Man

Lesley Ramsay

I t is the central idea of this book that what every woman really needs is a man. Not just any man, but *the* man – Jesus Christ.

What is it about this man that attracts such a bold assertion?

Outrageous claims

There are, first of all, his extreme claims. At different times, he asserted that he was the 'bread of life' (in other words – the great life satisfier), the 'light of the world' (the one who brings meaning to this seemingly chaotic universe), the giver of eternal life and, most remarkably, that he was God in the flesh.

So outrageous are these claims that we have only a few options open to us. The great English writer, C. S. Lewis, wrote:

> *"A man who was merely a man and said the sorts of things Jesus said would not be a great moral teacher. He would either be a lunatic – on the level with the man who says he is a poached egg – or else he would be the Devil of Hell. You must make a choice. Either this man was, and is, the Son of God: or else a madman or something worse. You can shut him up as a fool, you can spit at him and kill him as a demon. Or you can fall at his feet and call him Lord and God. But let us not come with any patronising nonsense about his being a great human teacher. He has not left that open to us. He did not intend to."*[1]

Anybody can make claims about themselves, but Jesus validated his claims by his actions. If you had walked that small strip of real estate known to us as Palestine two thousand years ago, you could have seen him heal men and women with leprosy with just a touch, or make a dangerously-ill child well with just a word. You could have seen him stop a storm, or bring back to life a young man on his way to his own funeral.

Extraordinary death

The way he lived was extraordinary; but it is the manner of his death that takes our breath away.

Thanks to Mel Gibson's film, *The Passion of the Christ,* we are well aware of the physical suffering that Jesus endured on the cross. But is that all that was going on in Jerusalem all those years ago?

This man was not just a martyr. In fact, from the moment we first encounter Jesus as an adult, we are left in no doubt that this death is his goal and purpose. Why would someone predict his own death and then do nothing to avoid it? On the contrary, he appears to willingly move towards it. Why?

The short answer is: God's love for both justice and us.

God's love for justice: Throughout this book we have talked at length about our rejection of God. We have described it as going our own way, turning our backs on him, divorcing God. It is about the rebellion of humanity against the rightful king of the universe.

The resulting mess in our world is enormous. In the macro, we pollute and make war. In the micro – in our personal relationships – we hurt and are hurt.

But worst of all is our separation from the One who made us and loves us. What we need to know more than anything else is that God is rightfully offended about the way we have treated him. And he can't just sweep our rebellion under the carpet.

There is real anger when it is reported serious criminals go free because of some loophole in the law. Guilty people deserve punishment. And so it is with God and us. The Bible describes God as someone who hates what is wrong and loves what is right. So he must deal with us justly. We deserve God's punishment for our rebellion.

God's love for us: What is he to do, then? God grieves over what this 'sin' had done to us. He really does care. And so his love drives him to act.

God's love for justice and us meet in his son, Jesus. When Jesus willingly went to his death, God's justice was satisfied. We are the ones who deserved death and condemnation, but Jesus, the perfect one, took our place. God placed the punishment for all the rebellion of all mankind on Jesus' broad shoulders.

Why? So that we, the guilty, could go free. It was the only way we could have forgiveness. See how much he loves us!

Most of us have experienced love in some relationship. My Mum and Dad were the first to love me; now I have a husband and children who love me. We expect our family and friends to love us! But God *shouldn't* love us, because we haven't loved him. And yet the crucifixion of Jesus reminds us of the breadth and enormity of God's love.

You can see why the death of Jesus is so important to Christians – it lies at the very heart of our relationship to God. Without it we could never hope to be forgiven or secure in our friendship with Him.

Unique resurrection

But the death of Jesus was not the end of the story. Three days later, his grave was empty and over the next couple of weeks, hundreds saw him walking around Jerusalem. God had raised him from the dead, never to taste death again. It is called the resurrection.

These days the word 'unique' has been debased – we hear of a 'unique television event' almost every second night. But this was *unique*. It literally had never happened before.

This rising from the dead is important for three reasons.

Firstly, it is God's stamp of approval on Jesus' sacrifice. If he had not risen from the dead, then his death would merely have been... well, just another death. But God is saying to the world, "This death worked! You can be sure of it because death could not hold him down".

Secondly, it guarantees new life lived forever in eternity for those who trust him. Do you remember Debbie's mum? She lives right now in the presence of God, because Jesus conquered death. It is a sad and miserable existence to believe that death is the end. We are born, we live, we work, we die. Is that all? Then life is meaningless! But God is saying to the world, "I ache to bring you home to live with me. And my son's resurrection from the dead means I can do it for you, too".

And thirdly, it is important because God has declared Jesus as Lord and Judge of this world. The Bible says:

> *God commands all people everywhere to repent. For he has set a day when he will judge the world with justice by the man he has appointed. He has given proof of this to all men by raising him from the dead.*[2]

Right now, 'the man' is 'the King'. He will judge with compassion and mercy. And he will judge *with* justice. God is saying to this world, "My Son is in charge. Don't ignore him. The consequences are terrifying".

One question remains: If Jesus is King and Judge, what will you do with him? If you have come to the conclusion that you really do **need** Jesus, you have come to a good place. But before you read the concluding chapter, let me explain one more thing.

Your response

I do not want you to think that this relationship with God that we have been talking about is automatically yours. God wants more than anything for you to have it. But there is a response you need to make. It is what the Bible calls repentance. Because you have so offended God, you can do nothing else but apologise for your appalling attitude and behaviour, beg his forgiveness, and determine to live a changed life from this point forward. Then you rely on Jesus' death to 'rescue' you, bringing you into a lifelong friendship with the Father.

Repentance is like doing a complete U-turn in the traffic and going in the opposite direction. It is a change of attitude towards God, which results in a change of behaviour. For Lauren and Rod, it meant giving up drugs and sleeping together. For Christine, it meant that she would have to treat men differently. For Isobel, it meant turning her back on the influence of friends who were pulling her away from her Christian faith. For Debbie, it was giving up her stubborn will and admitting her 'goodness' would get her nowhere with God.

But it is important to grasp this point – it is not a change of behaviour or lifestyle for its own sake. It is first and foremost a radical transformation of our approach to God. A changed life flows from here.

Is repentance hard? Yes. But as Lauren and Rod shared, nothing could make them go back to their old life. Their new life was infinitely better than they could ever imagine.

What will *your* response be? Read on…

ENDNOTES
1. C.S.Lewis, *Mere Christianity*
2. Acts 17:30-31

Conclusion
Di Warren

What women really need...

The hairdryer falls into the bath, there's an electric shock and advertising hot-shot Nick Marshal (Mel Gibson) suddenly has the ability to read the mind of any woman. He now knows 'what women want'. But does he know what we need? In fact, do we even know?

Open up any flashy catalogue and our 'wish list' grows, but so does our unrest with life. Such are our designer lives in the 21st Century… We know what we want, but what do we fundamentally **need**? What is at the core of our existence? What is the purpose of life?

The claim throughout this book is that **Jesus Christ** is what every women needs.

It's a tantalising claim. Could it be true? Is it possible that the search for meaning is over – that we need look no further than Jesus?

The writers of this book bear testimony to the fact that one man is able to meet their deepest need. Jesus is the answer to our longing for acceptance, certainty, clarity, compassion, contentment, control, forgiveness, love, relationship, satisfaction, security, spirituality, stability and truth. In fact, he can even read our mind!

You may still have questions about Jesus

It's very easy to find out more:

1. Buy a Bible from any major book store. The most popular translation is the *New International Version*. The four biographies of Jesus – Matthew, Mark, Luke and John – are the best place to begin reading .

2. Find a Bible teaching meeting. Ask a Christian friend, or contact The Good Book Company (see contact details at the end of this chapter) for churches in your local area or meetings in your work place, university, or school.

You may be ready to know Jesus right now

This is the most important decision you'll ever make, and yet it's also the hardest.

Here's what it's all about:

1. **Admitting sin**

   Up till now you have lived your whole life the wrong way – as if you are God and life is all about fulfilling your wants and desires. You have ignored and offended the true God and deserve his anger and judgment. You need to decide that this is the end of that way of living.

2. **Accepting Jesus as Saviour**

   In the 1st Century, God lovingly sent his Son Jesus to die in your place on the cross. He paid for your sin so forgiveness is now possible.

3. **Accepting Jesus as Lord**

   Jesus rose from the dead and is now in control of this whole world. Life is about bringing glory and honour to him, and awaiting his return to take you to heaven.

How do you become a Christian?

You need to say to God:

Dear God,

I am sorry for living my life as if I am more important than you.

Thank you for sending Jesus to die for me so that I can be forgiven and know you.

From this moment on, please help me to live with you as my God.

Amen.

What next?

The most important thing to know is that if you sincerely uttered this prayer then God has already answered it. You may not feel different, but you have just become a Christian – you have entered a new relationship with God through Jesus.

Now it's very helpful to get some encouragement and advice from another Christian. Why don't you speak to a Christian friend (perhaps the person who gave you this book)? Or you could contact us to help you find a local church where you can discover more about what it means to follow Jesus Christ.

The Good Book Company
Elm House, 37 Elm Road
New Malden
Surrey KT3 3HB
admin@thegoodbook.co.uk
Tel: 0845 225 0880

About the *authors*

Jennie Baddeley works in an 'office under the stairs'. She feels a bit like Harry Potter! Jennie enjoys relaxing after a busy day by listening to classical music, reading and spending time with her husband, Mark.

Angela Cole is a freelance journalist. She does some work from home while looking after her three young children by relying on husband, Nick, and burning the midnight oil.

Gillian Davis lives with her husband, Brett, and three kids in a fantastic wooden cottage near the beach which Brett built with his own hands! She loves honesty, laughter and teaching in a high school.

Red Fulton loves having long bubble baths, going to the hairdresser's and eating rich chocolate ice cream. However, she spends most of her time caring for her husband, Craig, and two children, who always keep her smiling.

Narelle Jarrett is the principal of a college that trains women for Christian ministry. She first wondered about God when she was three and unexpectedly found her questions answered twenty years later when she was introduced to Jesus.

Christine Jensen and her husband have five married children and are beginning to lose count of the number of grandchildren! Her special interest is children's literature, her favourite book being *The Best Christmas Pageant Ever.*

Sarie King was born in the UK, given a South African name and raised in Australia. Formerly a primary teacher, she now lectures in a women's college. She loves movies, beaches and bush.

Ruth Muffett trained as a social worker and is now a full-time mum. She loves swimming, but has swapped laps in the 'big pool' for sitting on the edge of the wading pool! You can still find her occasionally enjoying a Gloria Jeans' coffee.

Wendy Potts developed a passion for surfing as a teenager. She worked as a graphic designer before becoming a mum. She enjoys the beach with Shaun and their kids, the odd creative project, and good coffee on the verandah with friends.

Lesley Ramsay has come to the realisation that editing a book is no piece of cake! With her husband, she loves walking and holidays by the beach. On her own, she is into serious cappuccinos and reading thriller novels.

Jenny Salt used to be a nurse and flight attendant for Qantas. Now she lectures at a college. On weekends, she loves playing with her nieces and nephews, reading the newspapers over a cappuccino and watching movies with realistic endings.

Claire Smith originally worked in palliative care nursing, but is now studying for a PhD. She is married with a teenage son. To relax, Claire would rather walk along the beach than go to a coffee shop.

Michelle Underwood, a young mother, spends her day tripping over toys, smelling like vegemite sandwiches and wondering where all those odd stains come from. But she still enjoys Hollywood action movies and John Grisham novels.

Di Warren admits to enjoying maths, which she teaches casually at Sydney University. However, she can never remember her mobile number and loses her car keys most days. She loves her family, jazz music and *CSI*.